Theme Park

In the same series

Factory
Gillian Darley

Aircraft
David Pascoe

Dam
Trevor Turpin

Motorcycle
Steven E. Alford & Suzanne Ferriss

Bridge
Peter Bishop

School
Catherine Burke & Ian Grosvenor

Theme Park

Scott A. Lukas

REAKTION BOOKS

Published by Reaktion Books Ltd
33 Great Sutton Street
London EC1V 0DX, UK

www.reaktionbooks.co.uk

First published 2008
Transferred to digital printing 2012

Printed and bound by CPI Group (UK) Ltd, Croydon, CR0 4YY

British Library Cataloguing in Publication Data
Lukas, Scott A., 1968–
    Theme park. – (Objekt)
    1. Amusement parks   2. Amusement parks – Design and construction
    I. Title
    712.5

ISBN-13: 978 1 86189 394 9

Contents

Preface   7

1   Theme Park as Oasis   21

2   Theme Park as Land   65

3   Theme Park as Machine   97

4   Theme Park as Show   134

5   Theme Park as Brand   172

6   Theme Park as Text   212

References   246

Select Bibliography   260

Acknowledgements   262

Photo Acknowledgements   263

Index   265

Giant Ferris wheel, Yokohama Bay, Japan.

Preface

When you are inside a theme park, while you are watching one of its shows or spinning aboard one of its rides, you are thinking about the theme park, not about your humdrum life, relationship problems or issues with the boss at work. The whole idea of going to the theme park is that you can escape the problems of your everyday life and instead play in a virtual reality in which those problems are washed away and replaced with a world of immersion, joy, ecstasy and excitement. Since the proto-theme parks of Coney Island in the early 1900s people have been drawn to spaces that challenge everyday life, that overturn it and replace it, if only for a day. Today's theme park – whether a Disney or Universal theme park or a lifestyle- or boutique-themed space in Las Vegas – looks nothing like these early forms, yet it maintains something of the spirit of amusement parks like Coney Island, especially as it still provides people with an important outlet and diversion in an increasingly uprooted world.

Whether we love them or hate them, theme parks are increasingly ubiquitous throughout the world. Theme parks have wrongly been seen by many as superficial forms of culture – as places where people go to do things that don't matter much in the grand scheme of things and thus which amount to inconsequential spaces. In fact theme parks represent extraordinary spatial and social forms, they offer some of the most basic needs, reflect deep and powerful emotions and cognitive modes, and present some of the most telling and controversial representations of the world. Unlike cinema and theatre, in which audience members passively watch the action on the screen or stage, and unlike the narratives of television and books, which are static, the theme park uses the immersion of the individual inside an unfolding and evolving drama as the basis of its unique form. The theme park, as it expands beyond its proper site – as an enclosed space that contains thrill rides, shows, restaurants and food, and other attractions that are all tied to thematic landscapes that reflect our most popular fantasies – becomes a fully-fledged social and architectural form that continues to impact more and more people throughout the world, even if they do not realize it.

This book grows from my interest in understanding the contemporary theme park and the ways in which it emerged as a persuasive architectural and entertainment form. Since an early age I have been fascinated by theme parks. I visited them with friends and family as a child, and later in life I worked as an employee trainer at a major theme park. My interest in this form is both personal and academic. One of my prevailing concerns with the theme park is the difficulty of defining it. As much as it would seem that such a popular form of entertainment should be definable, I shall attempt to illustrate that the theme park often eludes our attempts to understand it. When you are walking in a theme park or quasi-theme park, you may hear claims that it is or is not a theme park, and may commonly hear journalists and critics referring to a space – however un-theme park it actually is – as a theme park. Though the word 'theme park' is used freely in everyday conversations, we may be referring to an amusement park, a high-tech museum or a shopping centre, and this attests to the way in which the theme park has entered our lives and our consciousness in intimate ways. As architectural objects theme parks are solidified forms, but as imaginative objects they are ephemeral, gaseous, rhizomatic, especially as they playfully move throughout our minds, hearts and relationships. And, throughout the world, the theme park has spread as a form. As it infiltrates more spaces – shopping malls, Las Vegas casinos, restaurants and other spaces – it expands beyond its earlier architectural, material and cultural form and becomes a form of life itself, ironically surpassing itself as an object and becoming indistinguishable from everyday life. As more people move in the world they become part of an ideological theme park. Moving through theme parks in the 3D virtual world of Second Life (www.secondlife.com) and on the Internet, interacting with others in scripted and dramaturgical consumer spaces, and even in decorating their homes in thematic ways, people have come together in a new and ironic world that is, itself, a theme park.

This book addresses the theme park in six interconnected senses. First, I emphasize the theme park as a fledgling form in early pleasure gardens, world's fairs, and the amusements of Coney Island, New York. During the late nineteenth and early twentieth centuries, amusement parks like Sea Lion Park, Steeplechase Park, Luna Park and Dreamland left indelible marks on the American populace. In its infant form the theme park provided citizens with an oasis away from the confines of everyday life. The next two chapters address the emergence of the theme park as a place – particularly Six Flags Over Texas and Disneyland – and the theme park as a machine. In this latter sense I focus on the proliferation of amusement machines in theme parks and how theme parks used the success of early amusement park experiments with machines to achieve phenomenal corporate success in the present. I then emphasize the theme park as a show, a form of never-ending entertainment in which all desires are met and the theme park acts as a performance about and through people. The book then moves to the theme park as a brand or commodity form to analyse the ways in which the contemporary, global theme park is primarily a corporate enterprise – one that is marketed across multiple forms of cross-promotion, and uses complex new forms of architecture and the senses to express itself. The text concludes with a discussion of the theme park as a text. Theme parks are not simply architectural or physical spaces, they are places of the mind that capture our attention in varied forms, including novels, feature films, video games and other virtual spaces.

The genesis of the theme park, metaphorically, emerges in the prehistoric caves of Europe. In caves like those of Lascaux two significant architectural forms emerge, simultaneously, the utilitarian and the symbolic. As I shall illustrate with the theme park there is a significant moment in prehistory in which spaces of function and spaces of symbol are fused. In today's theme park people can eat and socialize with family and friends, all the while partaking in heart-pounding rides and wandering through symbolic landscapes of pirates, the Old West and lush tropical isles. Throughout the book I will play off of the tension between utilitarian and symbolic space, and address the ways in which the theme park is the only consumer space that effectively manages this tension. All entertainment plays through aspects of this divide, but only the theme park can manage it in fully immersive, corporeal and psychologically intense ways. In visiting a movie theatre, for example, one sits in a utilitarian seat, but the primary mode of entertainment is a symbolic one on the screen. The moviegoer is further removed from the film in an interactive sense. In a theme park one partakes in an immersive experience and moves seamlessly from

utilitarian moments to symbolic ones. A major foundation of the theme park form is the continuous opportunity for immersion of the patron in all of the activities around her. It is a complete form.

The World's Columbian Exposition of 1893 provided a powerful glimpse of what a theme park could be. This, perhaps the most important of the world's fairs, was a first in many respects. Like the pleasure gardens of London such as Vauxhall and Ranelagh, the Prater of Vienna, Copenhagen's Tivoli and Jones's Wood in the United States, the Columbian Exposition offered varied entertainment within a managed space but, unlike them, it contained a midway in which attractions and sideshows intermingled with patrons, it premiered the famous Ferris wheel and it created thematic space – including varied displays of foreign people and architectural recreations of Cairo, Ireland, Germany and Algeria. What this and later world's fairs offered was the all-encompassing

In the 'Theme Park Cave' (Thad Donovan), two symbolic worlds collide in an unlikely way.

entertainment venture in which utilitarian pleasures like amusement rides were fused with symbolic and imaginative properties of people and places that connoted difference from fairgoers and, perhaps most significant for the evolution of theming, they showed that people could visit other places while staying in one spot – essentially, travelling without having to travel. Though not a theme park the World's Columbian Exposition provided an important leisure foundation that would lead to an amusement park boom in the United States, including the proto-theme parks at Coney Island and thousands of other regional and trolley parks. As theme parks grew in popularity in the 1950s and onwards, many parks, including Disneyland, Six Flags Over Texas and Knott's Berry Farm, became themed. One or more prevailing themes was used to create an ambience and a feeling of being

View of the Lapland Village (Midway Plaisance), 1893 World's Columbian Exposition: an exotic foreign space is brought home.

transported to another place or time. During the 1980s the theme park spread as a worldwide form, and soon theme parks were found in all of Europe, Asia, South Africa and Latin America. In the new millennium some of the most intensive developments of the theme park are taking place in China, Japan and Dubai.

Some contemporary critics have called some shopping malls 'theme parks', but this usage, as this book argues, is not entirely accurate. Just as the very first pleasure gardens, world's fairs and Coney Island amusement parks were not theme parks – though they had elements that would give form to today's theme park – contemporary examples of themed spaces, like shopping malls, restaurants and hotels are not necessarily theme parks. As the theme park spreads, like any consumer form, it will infect the world around it. More and more shopping malls and even museums use aspects of theme park architecture (including theming), interactive technologies and other elements to widen the appeal of their services and products. In the future, as increasing numbers of consumer venues use such approaches and as more of these venues move towards sensory marketing and become 'third spaces', it may be impossible to distinguish between theme parks, video arcades, shopping malls and other spaces. As the theme park continues to move, mutate and develop, like the rides and attractions that enthrall those who visit it, its form will come to dominate more and more of the world. Even in spaces removed from thematic emphases, the home, city streets and on the television channels of CNN, BBC and others, the world takes on the dynamics of a theme park. Far more than a metaphor, the theme park restructures the way the world operates and how we move within it. Even if we choose to avoid the theme park, because of its proliferation throughout the world we may find that we are living in one.

By 2006 13 of the top 25 highest attendance theme parks in the world existed outside the United States.[1] Theme parks are no longer strictly American phenomena, and now there are major theme parks in most countries of Europe and Asia and many Latin American nations. Throughout the world the theme park has expanded as a model that brings with it both a predictability of form and function – such as forced perspectives of buildings, clean streets and performative work – and a burgeoning of new and local forms of culture within its spaces. In the United States while the Disney and Six Flags models have expanded (offering efficiency, cleanliness, safety, predictability and variety entertainment), as have their associated brands and forms of marketing synergy, some traditional amusement parks that minimize their use of theme lands and theming have also prospered. Kennywood, Holiday World, Cedar Point and Knoebels emphasize their historical construction, their association with family and forms of kinship, their offering of kinetic thrills and rides and overall a less corporate focus. In the United States major theme parks, including Alton Towers, often play on the ideas of US models but more traditional parks like Blackpool Pleasure Beach, which includes numerous

Coney Island beach and boardwalk scenes, 1898, suggesting that anything was possible in a leisure space.

references to history and a distinctively non-corporate emphasis, have provided a different model that could ultimately impact the theme park's dominance. In a more focused way Camelot Theme Park uses the fantasy world of knights, Merlin and the Round Table to emphasize a more specific theming that is increasingly popular throughout the world. Even spaces of history and education like Eden Camp (Malton, North Yorkshire) and Jorvik Viking Centre in York use elements of the theme park to deliver a unique and perhaps controversial form of popular entertainment.

In Mexico some notable theme park chains like Six Flags have brought the corporate theme park to millions of Mexicans, and more traditional parks like La Feria de Chapultepec Mágico feature Aztec theming, thrilling roller coasters and traditional performances. Many new hybrid spaces also challenge the traditional construction of the theme park. Kidzania, a model also exported to Japan, has been received with popularity; in this version of a theme park children act out grown-up roles in the simulated space of a city, while their parents watch from balconies. Even more curious, a controversial space dubbed 'Migrant Mountain' at Eco Alberto Park simulates the experience of being an illegal immigrant and being captured by the police while trying to cross the border. Though not a theme park, this simulated experience owes much to the legacy of the theme park as a site of recreation, historical referencing and simulated experience.[2] Throughout Latin America, like much of the world, the theme park will continue to be a popular form that develops with the spread of Western-style consumer capitalism.

Like most of Europe, Germany has seen the expansion of corporate theme parks like Legoland Germany, as well as parks that cater exclusively to parents and their children (Ravensburger Spieleland, Playmobil FunPark). Major theme parks include Holiday Park (which features Western-style thrill rides), Heide-Park (which includes a pirate-themed hotel, Hotel Port Royal and a replica of the Statue of Liberty), Phantasialand (which references multiple cultures and fantasy worlds, including Africa, Native Americans, Atlantis, Colorado, China, Mexico, ghost towns, Hollywood, Aztecs and others), Europa-Park (which includes over fourteen theme lands, including an 'England' with a re-creation of the famous Globe Theatre and a football-themed hall of fame and interactive sports complex) and Movie Park Germany (whose tag-line is, 'Wow, I'm in the Movies!'). In France two of the most popular theme parks include Disneyland Resort Paris, which in its original form angered many French for its importing of American icons and corporate forms, and Parc Astérix, a mythological park that looks nothing like the corporate Disney park. Throughout Europe the theme park continues to express itself in interesting and diverse ways: in Austria, the Roman-archaeological edutainment area Archäologischer Park Carnuntum; in Belgium, the park based on the popular singer Bobbejaanland; in Italy, Italia in Miniatura offers miniature recreations of Italian landmarks, much like the popular form of miniature-based parks in Asia; PortAventura in Spain features atmospheric theme lands that reference Mexico, China, Polynesia and the Wild West; and Efteling in The Netherlands features intricately built attractions and buildings and whimsical cartoon characters.

In the United Arab Emirates Ski Dubai illustrates a trend, popular in Japan as well, of allowing people to partake in outdoor activities indoors and at Universal City Dubailand (opening 2010), the popular Universal movie brand will bring experiences and attractions familiar to people in the United States, while Global Village offers the cuisine, dances and sights of nearly 30 world cultures, suggesting that theme parks can provide people with the experience of seeing multiple cultures in one place. Dreamworld in Australia offers extensive animal exhibitions and attractions, something that Disney also capitalizes on at Animal Kingdom in Orlando, Florida. Like many resorts, The Lost City, part of South Africa's Sun City resort, offers an intense mythological construction of a lost, exotic and ultimately consumable past designed by Sol Kerzner, who also constructed the theme park-like casino and water park Atlantis in the Bahamas. The theme park Gold Reef City includes a melange of attractions unlikely to be found in other theme parks: a casino; food, dance and music of traditional African cultures; a museum on the history of apartheid; a heritage tour; and an underground mine attraction.

Throughout China major theme parks, shopping malls and historical reconstructions like World Park give patrons the opportunity to travel without travelling. In many venues people are given the sights, sounds, smells, performances and architecture of far-off lands, allowing them to take part in the global phenomenon of 'seeing the world' within the confines of one place. Numerous place-based attractions – including Shenzhen's Interlaken, a Swiss-based park; Greek villas in Beijing; a Weimar Village in Shanghai; Shenzhen's Window of the World; the planned Spaceport Shenyang; Beijing's Egyptian Theme Park; Wild Animal Park in Shanghai; and Minsk World theme park in Shenzhen, which includes a Soviet aircraft carrier – complement China's growing list of traditional theme parks like Happy Valley and Fantasy Land.[3] In Japan, Tokyo Disneyland, Universal Studios Japan and Tokyo DisneySea all illustrate that the American model of the corporate theme park, with its technological, branded and consumer tendencies, has popular applications outside the United States. Japan has shown some of the most interesting and hybrid spaces that draw on the technologies of theme parks. Some are

explicit, like Nagasaki's Huis Ten Bosch where Holland is re-created in striking detail, others are lifestyle spaces (the now-closed Miyazaki Ocean Dome) that provide traditional outdoor activities like skiing and surfing within indoor climate-controlled spaces.[4] As all these parks illustrate, in the world at large 'eclecticism is the degree zero of contemporary general culture', and it is the theme park that best exemplifies this trend.[5]

While developing research for this book, I came across a curious circumstance that further illustrates my sense that theme parks are peculiar objects, ones that are received in different ways by the public and ones that elude easy definition. In my previous studies of popular culture – including the controversial Hummer motor vehicle – I discovered that certain objects were subject to condemnation by the public.[6] Whether people had any contact with the objects or not, they seemed to have strong opinions about them. During conversations with individuals in Las Vegas about the legacy of the theme park, I was told by some that Vegas,

Nagasaki's Huis Ten Bosch, where Holland is recreated in striking detail.

much to my surprise, had no elements of the theme park in it and that people who work in the city make an effort to distinguish it from a theme park – it is not, above all, an 'adult theme park' as many people have claimed. In further conversations with American museum officials, I found a similar distancing from the theme park. Statements like 'we must distinguish ourselves from theme parks' were common, and it made me wonder why something as influential as the theme park should be viewed as such an illicit cultural object. While conversing with a number of these officials, I tried to paraphrase Siegfried Kracauer's concept of history from 'The Mass Ornament':

> The position that an epoch occupies in the historical process can be determined more strikingly through an analysis of its inconspicuous surface-level expressions than from that epoch's judgments about itself. Since these judgments are expressions of the tendencies of a particular era, they do not offer conclusive testimony about its overall constitution. The surface-level expressions, however, by virtue of their unconscious nature, provide unmediated access to the fundamental substance of the state of things.[7]

My sense of trying to reference Kracauer's 'inconspicuous surface-level expressions' of the theme park – as they now exist in Las Vegas casinos and in contemporary interactive museums – reflects my interest in addressing the theme park not as a solid object (as these many officials and even laypersons would like) but as a gaseous one, as a thing that affects the world with varying consequences. In this way, when we visit a contemporary museum and we notice an interactive display for children that looks like a play area from an amusement or theme park, or when we walk into a modern casino and we see the re-creation of a far-off land that looks like the theming of Coney Island-era parks, we see the remnants of history, the origins of the theme park peeking through at us in the present. Whether we like what we see or not is open to debate, but the legacy of the theme park, like that of consumerism and popular amusements in general, is profoundly and widely felt.

1 Theme Park as Oasis

Hell is constructed of papier-mâché, and painted dark red. Everything
in it is on fire – paper fire – and it is filled with the thick, dirty odor of
grease. Hell is very badly done.
Maxim Gorky, on a visit to Coney Island.[1]

With his description of Coney Island, Maxim Gorky, the famous
Marxist literary figure, launched one of the first polemics against
the amusement park industry. Gorky's words reflect an almost surrealistic description of Coney Island, as he writes of animal shows
and varied attractions like Hell Gate and The Flood. Everywhere he
finds what he detests, the 'glittering boredom' and the 'varied
boredom' that characterize ride after ride and show after show.
Like Tolstoy's criticism of the 1893 World's Columbian Exposition,
Gorky fears the character of the amusements being proffered at
Coney Island, yet he is also fascinated by it. Unlike Tolstoy he
directly assaults the major foundation of amusement and theme
parks – artifice. Pre-dating the post-1960s critiques of the
'Disneyization' (or 'Disneyfication') caused by the theme park
industry, Gorky pinpoints one of the most significant relationships
in the theme park, that between the artificial and the real.

Since Plato's powerful image of the cave in *The Republic* people have been simultaneously trapped between the varying poles of
the artificial and the real. And since cave art in prehistoric times
people have been comfortable with the uneasy play between the
real and the unreal. In the case of the contemporary theme park this
idea has been widely expressed, if not overstated. Like Plato's cave,
theme parks provide the powerful illuminations of architecture,

rides, shows and varied entertainment that cast shadows on and affect the people who visit them. What is debatable is what the effect of theme park amusements on people is. Is it slavish consumerism, as Gorky would have it, or is it meaningful, often nostalgic and joyful, as many who have visited theme parks would have it? Do the simulated architectural worlds of theme parks reflect who we are? To be able to deal with the contradictions of the artificial and the real, it would seem, is an essence of understanding the nature of any theme park.

Well before Gorky's diatribe against Coney Island powerful forms of artificiality that challenged the real and provided a refuge or oasis in contrast with the chaos of the outside world were taking root. These forces led to the emergence of the theme park but, as we shall see, they look nothing like the theme parks of the contemporary world. Throughout this book I hope to show that, contrary to attempts to trace a clear path from earlier amusement traditions like fairs and world expositions to the contemporary theme park, there is no linear path from these early amusements

The Dragon's Gorge Scenic Railway at Luna Park offered fantasy escapism and thrilling propulsion of the body.

to their later kin. Instead we must understand the trajectory of the theme park in the form of historical whispers, thematic shouts in the night and rhizomatic influences of direction and misdirection. Like Jacques Derrida's 'différance' the traces of the theme park, as much as they resemble the amusements of the past, are indirect. In the case of the earliest traces of the theme park we discover a significant architectural construction of the artificial-real.

The earliest of dwellings, whether adobe huts or early settlements, establish the important principle of the zone. Etymologically, zone refers to climatic regions of the earth, or to regions that are 'distinguished from adjacent regions by some special quality or condition'.[2] In the case of natural climatic zones there is no human intervention in the distinguishing of the zone, but in geography and architecture the 'special quality or condition' is determined by humans. With the earliest pleasure gardens, including Vauxhall Gardens, Ranelagh Gardens and Jenny's Whim of London, the Prater of Vienna, Tivoli of Copenhagen and the picnic groves of the United States, including Jones's Wood, the theme park emerges in the lush gardens and natural outdoor spaces that were landscaped, modified and connected to the pleasures of people. The utilitarian features of the landscape are combined with the altered features of entertainment geography and architecture. What early leisure gardens establish is not simply that humans may inhabit the land, but that they may modify it in synthetic ways that perfectly fuse the natural and the unnatural. The theme park, rather than being an unnatural abomination on the landscape, is a fusion of the utilitarian and the symbolic, the natural and the unnatural.

Vauxhall Gardens opened in the mid-nineteenth century and is considered by some to be the 'first internationally famous pleasure garden'.[3] At Vauxhall variety entertainment – including acrobatic performances, fireworks, dancing, music and food – was the norm.

In 1728 a 'season ticket' was developed that allowed people to visit the gardens throughout the year.[4] Spectacle, which would become the standard at amusement parks at Coney Island, was established with performances that included aeronauts descending from balloons and unfortunately included the death of one such performer.[5] At a number of the gardens spectacles included performances like the re-creation of the Battle of Waterloo and the eruption of Mount Etna.[6] This tradition of spectacle performance would later come full circle at Coney Island. London's Ranelagh Gardens, popular in the mid-1700s, included lavish architectural features, such as a giant rotunda and a Chinese house, and offered games of chance to the public. During the years of Ranelagh's prominence, the fireworks display became a staple of outdoor pleasure gardens, including at the Marylebone Gardens of London.[7] Like the technological displays that take place in many theme and amusement parks of the

The roller coaster, though a synthetic and unnatural projection of human desire, must situate itself within nature.

present, fireworks provided the public with a pyrotechnic show that was unmatched at the time. The popularity of pleasure gardens like those of Vauxhall led to illegitimate franchising of the gardens. At least five 'Vauxhall Gardens' appeared in New York.[8] A similar, also illegitimate transfer of the successful franchises of Coney Island amusement parks would take place in the United States in the early 1900s, as would later a counterfeit version of Disneyland at Shijingshan Amusement Park in Beijing, China and the now-closed Nara Dreamland in Japan. What such copying suggests is the emergence of an amusement tradition that, like the theme park, would be an immensely popular enterprise.

At Jenny's Whim, established in London in 1750, the lushness of the natural landscape was complemented with artificial means of amusement. Mechanical mermaids, fish and monsters were brought to mechanical life at a pond in the park.[9] At Jenny's Whim the use of special effects in the form of primitive animatronics established the important theme park technology of cybernetics, in which special effects and mechanical operations are used as entertainment interaction between patrons and the artificial.[10] The Prater of Vienna, opened in 1766, provided another important impetus for the theme park. In addition to swings and primitive amusement rides, the Prater featured varied concessions, including stands that sold sausages.[11] Similar to the later parks of Coney Island, the amusement zones of the Prater emphasized the participation of mixed social classes in the various forms of entertainment.[12] Like the Prater the Tivoli of Copenhagen used the natural environment to create a unique amusement space for patrons. At Tivoli plants, buildings and entertainment areas fashioned a spatial division that would come full circle in the contemporary theme park, in which further spatial distinctions of theme lands are created.

Speaking of Tivoli, its architect George Carstensen offered that 'Tivoli will never, so to speak, be finished'.[13] Like the flux that characterized the updating of the many amusement parks of Coney Island, Tivoli established the idea that a successful theme park must be continually updated. In fact, years later, Walt Disney stated that 'Disneyland will never be completed. It will continue to grow as long as there is imagination left in the world.' The key way in which the pleasure garden affects the future and makes way for the theme park is the principle of multi-use entertainment space. The contemporary theme park is a holistic fusion of rides, shows, concessions and attractions. Whereas other forms of popular entertainment are conditioned by their nature – a cinema can generally only show motion pictures – the theme park, as influenced by the multi-use entertainment space of the pleasure garden and later the

Tivoli (1860) and switchback railroad: an early form of the theme park begins to take shape.

world exposition tradition, provides the patron with everything. All desires are met, with the only limit being the patron's imagination and energy to partake in the amusements.

It is unlikely that a contemporary theme park visitor would consider any of the famous pleasure gardens of Europe to be theme parks; in fact, they were not theme parks, but elaborate natural settings in which some future features of the theme park can be located. More influential to the modern theme park is the world exposition or world's fair. While early pleasure gardens were limited in the amount of entertainment and variety amusement that could be provided, with world expositions, greater capital investment allowed more amusements and increased abundance. Populations expected superior attractions and more extravagant entertainment with each subsequent exposition. Within the amusement world of Coney Island, a similar expectation was created, in part fuelled by an amusement 'arms race' of sorts. As Dreamland helped illustrate, a penchant to copy popular attractions from one park, and in many cases make them bigger at the new park, soon became an amusement standard.[14] In today's theme park the emphasis on abundance continues. In some cases this occurs with amusement rides. Cedar Point, for example, can only claim to be the roller coaster capital of the world by constantly reinvesting in more roller coasters in its park, for all the while other theme parks attempt to catch up to claim this distinction. In the desire for more – whether rides, thematic vistas or shows – both an economic and a symbolic accumulation take hold in the theme park.

An important aspect that is heralded by the world's fair and later adopted in both the amusement park and theme park is the prominent role of commodity. Walter Benjamin, speaking of the 1867 Exposition Universelle in Paris, offered that the world expositions entertained 'by elevating people to the level of commodities'.[15] Like the trade fairs that preceded them world expositions relied on the commodity as a means of identity, and in the contemporary theme park the commodity has become the defining of all forms (see chapter Five). For the fairgoer attending an exposition meant not being an individual, but being part of a social drama of which commodity was both the catalyst and connector. Though some popular amusements, like cinema, are highly individualistic phenomena, the world's fair ushered in an age of social consumption in which fairgoers could delight in viewing commodities on display alongside others. The fair became a palace of consumption, a hyperreal oasis of goods. This is a key development that is taken to an extreme in the kinaesthetic thrills of Steeplechase Park, and later modified at Disney theme parks and quasi-theme parks in Las Vegas. On their surface world's fairs proclaim themselves to be complete entities, particularly as they display the commodities of architecture, technological invention and people themselves (in the case of anthropological displays). Yet, through their construction as complete spaces in and of themselves, world's fairs promoted the important theme park principle of the total package. World's fairs proved that through careful attention

View of Coney Island from the ocean (c. 1910), a sign of things to come in terms of the theme park and its impact on urbanization and sprawl.

to architecture, performance and symbolism an enclosed space could be completely distinguished from other spaces. Just as the city promoted a new vision of the world, the world's fair was 'designed for a new sensibility'.[16] While people never fully accepted the entertainments of the pleasure gardens as a new reality, with the world exposition a new tradition of the 'real' emerges.

Through their very design world's fairs created distinctive entertainment zones with 'clear boundaries . . . and coherence'.[17] The most famous of all of the expositions is perhaps the World's Columbian Exposition, held in Chicago in 1893. This world's fair was such a draw that many families spent their life savings and burial money just to attend, and it is reported that one person, so obsessed with making the pilgrimage to Chicago, walked the entire length of the railroad tracks from Houston. While all expositions are heralded for their revolutionary effects on architecture, technology,

The interior of the electricity building at night for the 1893 World's Columbian Exposition, illustrating how the commodity form would enter the theme park.

design and entertainment, the World's Columbian Exposition is unique in a number of respects. First, the 'White City' created architectural wonder on a scale rarely seen before, and that in part helped spur the City Beautiful movement. Second, it presented an optimistic and dominant view of the future and the role of America in it and did so in a manner that is reminiscent of later theme parks, especially those of Disney, and their elevation of the idea of the American dream.[18] Third, it projected a vision of the 'Other', of a racialized and spatialized person who is the subject of the gaze and reflection of the fairgoer (a trend that is picked up in later theme parks like Dollywood, Busch Gardens and Disney parks, as well as many parks in China such as the Chinese Ethnic Culture Park). Fourth, it offered the unprecedented Midway Plaisance – a site of amusement and wonder in which people could view re-created villages from around the world and exotic peoples in native dress, and which provided numerous restaurants and other attractions. Fifth, it created an impressive sanitation and utility system that, like the complex backstages of modern theme parks, provided drinking water, toilets and other necessities for patrons. Last, it established the dominance of the first major amusement ride at a world's fair – the Ferris wheel.

In many ways the World's Columbian Exposition was the world's first proto-theme park. Though it did not contain many of the elements that now define theme parks, it offered a powerful vision of what could be in terms of an all-encompassing, enclosed amusement space. As the 1893 exposition helps demonstrate, one of the most notable architectural aspects of the world's fair was the attention to symbolism. The way in which each nation presented itself at the fair was through the realm of the symbolic, not the actual. The architecture of the exposition was 'used to connote symbolic meanings, minimizing its primary utilitarian functions'.[19]

The point of stressing the symbolic over the utilitarian and of using architecture in exaggerated and hyperbolic senses would come to influence both the Coney Island amusement park and the contemporary theme park. Many critics have decried this use of symbolic architecture, and in so doing they fail to understand the unique relationship of entertainment and architecture. The powerful symbolism of architecture and landscape at the world's fair created an important opportunity for the theme park to offer artifice that was meaningful to patrons. As Coney Island will demonstrate, especially Luna Park, much of the architectural symbolism taken from the world's fair was that not that which is functional, such as an agricultural building, but that which was extravagant, unreal and spectacular. In addition many of the world's fairs established iconic relationships between architecture and entertainment. At the 1939–40 New York World's Fair two prominent structures that were

The Windmills at the 1893 World's Columbian Exposition helped forge a tradition of eclectic and uncanny architecture that would dominate later theme parks.

simultaneously icons – the Trylon and the Perisphere – offered themselves as recognizable logos of the fair (arguably, the most recognizable icons from any fair). Other iconic architectural forms would later emerge in the examples of Cinderella Castle and Spaceship Earth at Disneyland and Epcot.

While pleasure gardens often only focused on the temporality of the present – with rare dabbling in the past through some historical recreations – the world's fairs effectively fused past, present and future. They highlighted what was desirable about present life, referenced the past in often nostalgic ways and piqued interest in a future that was purported to be coming. The future was especially interesting. In the case of expositions like the New York World's Fair of 1939–40 the future was equated with technologies of 'The World of Tomorrow'. Fairgoers were treated to Democracity, a 'perfectly integrated, futuristic metropolis pulsing with life and rhythm and music', housed inside the massive Perisphere building.[20] Predating both the architectural forms and prescriptive suggestions for how society should be at Disney's Epcot, Democracity offered the theme park a most powerful role: amusement could not only reflect the trends of society, but could offer new ones, suggesting visions of how society might look one day. Though many of Democracity's visions were not accurate – including its concept of orchards that housed individual umbrellas for each plant – some were, most notably its showcasing of an intercontinental highway system that would link America from coast to coast. It is not enough that this and other fairs showcased new technologies – a trend that theme parks revel in – what is more is that the fair took a bolder step in saying that it could, and through leisure, invent the future: 'Seldom, if ever, has such an entrancing vista been created by man. Visitors will never forget it, symbolic as it is of the interdependence of man with his fellow and of humanity's age-old quest for knowledge, increased leisure and happiness.'[21] Like Disney's Epcot and Universal Studios theme parks which followed, Democracity, in the official text from 1939, envisions a fully functioning world in which leisure is an equal partner with everyday life.[22] Amusement could now drive society, not the converse, and this drive that propels society forward is, as evidenced in the world's fair, a spatial and architectural one.

At the 1901 Pan-American Exposition in Buffalo, a year before the release of George Méliès' *A Trip to the Moon* (*Le voyage dans la Lune*) – a film that many consider to be the first science fiction film – architect and amusement entrepreneur Fred Thompson premiered one of the first dark simulation rides. Called A Trip to the Moon, Thompson's ride was a great success. Unlike previous attractions in which spectators watched the action on a stage, in this simulation, fairgoers actually moved and participated in a drama that unfolded around them. Passengers embarked on moonships with wings and then flew above Buffalo; passing through storms and clouds, they eventually landed on the moon, where they explored mysterious caverns, ate the green cheese of midget Selenites, and watched the dancing of moon maids.[23] Like Méliès' film, Thompson's trip was a journey of epic sensorial and corporeal proportions. His attraction was eventually moved to Georges Tilyou's Steeplechase Park, where it thrilled many more people and made large sums of money until it ended up at Luna Park. With the world's fair a new dimension of amusement emerges – a form of entertainment intertextuality in which the same or similar attraction is transported from the world's fair to an amusement or theme park. Thompson's Trip proved to be successful at the Pan-American Exposition, and it was thus ready made for a new audience at Coney Island. Later, at the 1964–5 New York World's Fair, Walt Disney produced four attractions, including It's a Small World, the

Carousel of Progress and Great Moments with Mr Lincoln (which would inspire the Hall of Presidents at Disneyland). These attractions became staples of Disney parks and they help demonstrate the processes of adaptation and citation that are common in the world of the theme park, especially in respect to rides and attractions. In some cases, citation was simply ripping off rides from one park and opening them up at the next, as in Dreamland's use of Luna's attractions.

Like the theme parks of the contemporary world, and rather like the amusement parks of Coney Island, world's fairs created an important distinction of space that further differentiates them from earlier regional fairs, trade fairs and pleasure gardens. Namely, they establish an overarching theme. Themes like 'The Century of Progress' (Chicago, 1933–4), 'The World of Tomorrow' (New York, 1939–40), 'The Confluence of Civilizations in the Americas' (San Antonio, 1968) and 'Energy Turns the World' (Knoxville, 1982) are examples of the ways in which world's fairs used overarching themes as a means of establishing both the cultural authority and the nationalistic identity of the fair. Later amusement parks like Steeplechase Park used looser themes, such as the 'funny place', to draw customers into the gates. It was not until the 1960s in the United States that theme parks revitalized the world's fair tradition of the overarching theme. As the next chapter illustrates, sometimes the main theme is subdivided into

The exterior of the famous 'A Trip to the Moon' ride at Luna Park illustrates the success of the theme park to take people on an other-worldly journey.

subthemes that elaborate on the main one or, in some cases, diverge from it. The theme park Dollywood uses the overarching theme of Dolly Parton's celebrity coupled with down-home, rustic Americana to provide a mountain oasis for patrons. Contemporary quasi-theme park spaces, such as Las Vegas casinos, in some cases use the overarching theme in ways more explicit than proper theme parks. With the overarching theme, the movement towards the theme park is one step closer.

While many of the pleasure gardens of Europe eventually closed, the world exposition suggested that, in theory, there could be a permanence to the impermanence of its entertainment. 'Residuals' or architectural and landscaping leftovers, like the Space Needle from the Century 21 Exposition in Seattle (1962), provided a permanent reminder of the amusements of the past. In theory the architectural and technological advances of the fairs could become permanent fixtures, if not symbols, for a community; they could also perhaps inspire economic stimulus for a community. But world's fairs were not always successful in this respect. The 1939–40 New York World's Fair included a parachute jump; it was later moved to Coney Island where it now stands dormant but is known to many as 'Brooklyn's Eiffel Tower'. The 1964–5 New York World's Fair saw most of its buildings and attractions recycled in other parts of the United States. By this time, the world's fair was losing popularity; fairs began to record losses, even bankruptcy, and with the advent of new forms of transportation – including air travel and the automobile – the world's fair lost its prominence.[24] The effort to record a permanent exhibition of popular amusements was left to the amusement parks, including those of Coney Island, New York.

Of the early influences on the theme park – including pleasure gardens, world's fairs and amusement parks – the most significant

The emblematic Parachute Jump at Coney Island, now inoperable (photographed in 2005).
A stark reminder of the impermanence of amusements.

of these are the parks of Coney Island. From 1895 to 1964, Sea Lion Park, Steeplechase Park, Luna Park and Dreamland established an agenda for the theme park that continues into the present. Ironically, many people know nothing of these prominent parks, which bespeaks the radical transformation that has occurred in modern amusements. Some fans consider parks like Luna to be the 'first Disneyland', or the 'Disneyland that should have been', and many consider the contemporary spectacles of Disney theme parks and Las Vegas quasi-theme parks to be rooted in the influences of Luna and Dreamland. Some believe that the amusement parks of Coney Island were the 'real thing' in terms of their emphasis on social mixing, entertainment for entertainment's sake and the avoidance of the corporatism and branding of contemporary theme parks. Part of this nostalgia, it seems, lies in the fact that Coney Island parks were amusement parks, not theme parks. With the launching of theme parks in the 1960s, the idea of one or more prominent themes carried throughout the entire amusement venue is initiated. Amusement parks, many of which still exist in the contemporary world, focus on exciting rides, amusing attractions and varied entertainment, but they do not pay significant attention to an overarching theme. Interestingly, contemporary theme parks owe the most to the amusement parks of Coney Island, in no small part due to the fact that these early amusement parks illustrate the idea that a theme park could be a total space. In piecemeal fashion, theme parks would borrow from the successes of these earliest amusement parks in the United States.

Like the world's fair, the early amusement space of Coney Island offered a geographical space in which varied public amusements could peacefully coexist. Among the early pre-amusement park attractions, two stand out. The steam-elevator-powered Iron Tower, a staple at the Centennial International Exhibition of 1876

(Philadelphia), was moved to Coney, while George Ferris' famous Ferris wheel of World's Columbian Exposition fame was rebuilt at one-half the size at Coney Island by its first entrepreneur George Tilyou in 1894. Both major attractions bring to the theme park an architectural form that is recognizable to the public – iconic in the sense of the many symbolic buildings of the world's fair. The Iron Tower provided a 300-foot view of the island, with panoramic views that were then unmatched, and was then the tallest structure in the United States. Like the careful attention to the field of vision and landscape in pleasure gardens the tower uses vision as an apparatus to generate amusement, but it does so with a twist. By merging height and field of vision the Iron Tower allows the amusement patron to see everything that is happening below. Just as the design of early pleasure gardens provided amusement vistas through the design of landscape and flora, the new emphasis on mechanical vistas did the same, albeit through a more artificial means. Similarly, Tilyou's Ferris wheel used height as it allowed riders to see the marvellous sights above the beaches of Coney, but he added the important element of kinetics which he would later exploit to more success in his dizzying rides at Steeplechase Park. Height and kinetics, merged in the architectural forms of amusement rides, provided Coney Island with an early identity that it would need for its expansion into the amusement park era.

The phrase, 'the apotheosis of the ridiculous', attributed to a visitor to Coney Island, for many summed up the varied attractions, architecture and amusements that made up the beachfront resort.[25] Early Coney Island displayed an eclecticism of entertainment, with saloons, gambling halls, brothels and other often seedy attractions spotting the landscape. With the addition of major architectural attractions like the Iron Tower and the Ferris wheel, Coney Island began to take on an identity. Hotels helped establish its transformation into a major amusement venue. By the 1870s three hotels – the Brighton Beach Hotel, the Manhattan Beach Hotel and the Oriental Hotel – adorned the beaches of Coney Island. Like the hotels that are partners to contemporary amusements at Disney and Universal parks and along the Las Vegas Strip, these hotels (though in some cases too expensive for them) gave beachgoers an opportunity to unwind between trips to the theatres and journeys along the sand. The most famous of the hotels, the Elephant Hotel (which was shaped like an elephant),

Though never constructed, the proposed 700-foot steel Globe Tower at Coney Island suggested an architectural and entertainment model for the theme park.

offered a glimpse of the iconic architecture that would eventually find its way to theme parks, major cities like Los Angeles that promoted roadside architecture and the casinos of the Las Vegas Strip. People often travelled to Coney just to catch a glimpse of the Elephant, leading to the phrase 'seeing the elephant', and with its building, the Elephant Hotel drew on the iconic architectural traditions common to the world expositions.[26] Later, the elephant appeared in other amusement parks throughout the United States, and not only did this symbol create instant mental associations with Coney Island, it allowed a certain tradition of the absurd and the surreal to take hold.[27]

The year 1867 was a significant one for Coney Island, for it was in this year that Charles Feltman combined a Vienna sausage and a Kaiser roll and produced the first 'hot dog', an equally iconic form. Later, in 1916, Nathan Handwerker would open Nathan's Famous and would help launch the popular Coney Island food haunt that is still open in 2008. The hot dog is the amusement park's first food form, and as other food revolutions in the theme park will illustrate (such as the themed restaurant), food is an intimate part of the corporeal appeal of the theme park. In 1877 an aquarium opened that featured animal performances and human freaks of nature, and soon mechanical amusement rides, including carousels and steam swings, began to adorn the beachfronts of Coney Island. In 1884 LaMarcus Thompson introduced the first Switchback Gravity Railroad (or roller coaster) at Coney. Revolutionary at this time, one observer wrote that, 'The Coney Island roller coaster is a contrivance designed to give passengers . . . all the sensations of being carried away by a cyclone, without the attendant sacrifice of life or limb.'[28] By 1890 Coney Island was known as the horse racing capital of the United States, a fact that George Tilyou would capitalize on at Steeplechase Park.[29]

Fireworks were also a regular act along the beach, and perhaps to a frequenter of the pleasure gardens of London, Coney Island would have appeared to be surprisingly similar but vaster in scale. An expanding American leisure population took advantage of the opportunity to mingle with others in carefree entertainments. A changing sexual code of conduct gave men and women an opportunity to partake in gaiety along the beach and within the many rides and attractions that literally threw them together. As people were propelled into further proximity with one another, the idea emerged that the amusement park itself could be a harbinger of democratic ideals:

> When you bathe in Coney, you bathe in the American Jordan. It is holy water. Nowhere else in the United States will you see so many races mingle in a common purpose for a common good. Democracy meets here and has its first interview, skin to skin. Here you find the real interpretation of the Declaration of Independence – the most good for the greatest number, tolerance, freedom.[30]

But soon the haphazard and sporadic attractions of Coney Island gave way to the era of the major amusement parks.

Known as the 'water god' and the 'fearless frogman', Captain Paul Boyton was a self-made hero. He reportedly helped blow up a Chilean vessel by swimming up to it and attaching a one-hundred-pound torpedo to its hull. Boyton was also known for his exploits as an explorer and daring 'stuntman', including demonstrations of his swimming prowess on the Thames, in the English Channel and on the Mississippi River. He also helped demonstrate a new aquatic lung invention. In 1895, riding the success of his celebrity, he opened Sea Lion Park in an area adjacent to the Elephant Hotel. Boyton 'was his own headline attraction', and this

fact created a link between the celebrity and the amusement park – a feat that would be repeated with Walt Disney at Disneyland, Dolly Parton at Dollywood and singer Bobbejaan Schoepen at Bobbejaanland in Belgium.[31] Sea Lion Park had an admission charge at the gate, a feature that later helped distinguish enclosed amusement parks from carnivals and sideshow strips.

Sea Lion's main attraction was the Shoot-the-Chutes, a water ride that propelled riders down a steep incline into a watery splash in a pond below. Boyton's ride was so successful that he eventually opened similar attractions in Chicago, Boston, Washington

Democracy's masses in a scene on the Bowery, Coney Island.

and San Francisco.[32] Like later theme park rides that resulted in spin-offs, most notably the Tower of Terror ride at numerous Disney parks, the Shoot-the-Chutes proved that a ride itself could be an amusement draw. Boyton also parlayed the powerful element of water – which in many people's minds connotes gaiety and adventure, propulsion and power, the unexpected and the reactionary – into an entire park themed around water. As one description of the Shoot-the-Chutes offered, 'Ladies screamed, children clung wildly to anybody within reach. One great shocking plunge, a leap in the air, a heaving and tossing, and the boat glided into the waters of the lake, to be brought to a safe landing.'[33] In the late twentieth century water would become the mainstay of theme parks (or water parks) such as the Wet & Wild chain and Schlitterbahn in the United States. In addition to the famous water ride that he premiered, Boyton offered a Flip-Flap roller coaster, cages of wild wolves and the uproarious shows of sea lions – the

Schlitterbahn, a contemporary example of Paul Boyton's earlier watery achievements.

creatures that gave name to his park. With these last elements Boyton further illustrated the tension between the natural and the unnatural, using sea creatures in combination with mechanical water rides to bridge the gap between the two realms. Like the later SeaWorld, Busch Gardens and Disney's Animal Kingdom the Captain offered the animal as a means to creating a hybrid zoo/theme park. Like the very first oasis – not the Garden of Eden but the prehistoric watering holes of Europe where humans and animals intermingled – Boyton created a new sort of oasis, one in which humans, the elements of nature and animals coexisted.

Prior to opening Steeplechase Park in 1897 George Tilyou operated a number of attractions along the boardwalk at Coney Island and worked in minor real estate deals. At one point he sold bottles of 'authentic beach sand' to gullible people from the Midwest.[34] Less of a celebrity and more of a showman and a marketer than Boyton – whose Sea Lion Park did not outlast the year 1902 – Tilyou used his insights about people and his ability to sell

An advertisement for Paul Boyton's Shoot-the-Chutes illustrates the revolution of water that would later lead to the popular water park.

a gimmick in ways that rivalled those of showman and circus entrepreneur P. T. Barnum. Tilyou was the theme park's first real entrepreneur and, more than any other innovator at Coney Island, focused on the explicit desires of the patron, an emphasis that would come to dominate the contemporary period of theme parks in which 'guests first' became the norm of both Disney and Six Flags theme parks.

Like Fred Thompson later at Luna Park Tilyou was attracted to the world exposition, which he saw as a proving ground for his own amusement ideals. In addition to his own smaller Ferris wheel Tilyou brought the famous Streets of Cairo and other re-creations from the World's Columbian Exposition to Coney. New to many, these 'themed' geographical attractions introduced the elements of the faux ethnological and the faux geographical to Coney Island. Unlike Sea Lion Park, which remained relatively static in its attractions, Tilyou was convinced that people needed to have their amusement desires met in as many and as varied

The mechanical horses on the tracks at Steeplechase Park, an unholy meeting of nature and culture.

ways as possible. He brought the popular A Trip to the Moon ride to his park for a year, and was willing to bring in new attractions and take down others so long as the result was the fulfilment of his patrons' desires. Unlike Luna Park and Dreamland with their focus on the grand and the sublime Tilyou emphasized the everyday, especially the ordinary person's body and its connection to the machine.

Tilyou's park was enclosed and, like the world's fair, Steeplechase demonstrates the importance of the berm – the enclosed amusement space that can be completely monitored and controlled by the operators. The enclosed park also gives the park operators a sense of identity; later this sense of geographical wholeness would lead to the modern theme park experience in which a theme park literally becomes a world in and of itself and in which theme lands become subdivisions of the park's corporate identity. Surrounding his park was Tilyou's 'theme' – the steeplechase. Tilyou discovered that the steeplechase ride – a mechanized horse race on tracks – was quite popular in England. Trying to counter the popularity of Boyton's Shoot-the-Chutes at Sea Lion Park, Tilyou brought the steeplechase ride to his park. The steeplechase was the central attraction of the park, and thus provided its name, as a sort of synecdoche. His choice of the steeplechase also related to Coney Island's status as the horse racing capital of the United States. Tilyou realized that the American amusement psyche was connected to the horse, and thus he wanted to embellish the psyche, or perhaps tap into it, by theming his park with the mechanized horse race. Much later, at Disney and Universal theme parks, the fascination with the motion picture would become a major component of the thematic apparatuses of theme park attractions like the motion simulator ride based on movies. In many ways Steeplechase proved the important point that the theme park could be the voice of the nation.

One of Tilyou's most revolutionary insights was the need to connect to the amusement imagination of the park patron. He created the famous 'funny face' that became Steeplechase's logo for over 65 years and, much like Walt Disney and Angus Wynne, Jr (of Six Flags) who followed him, he had a keen 'psychological insight' into the entertainment desires of the everyday person.[35] The first corporate logo of the theme park, Tilyou's funny face is an acknowledgement of the need to create immediate and unquestionable impressions on the customer. An even more revolutionary approach of Tilyou's Steeplechase was the emphasis on the mechanical amusement ride and its integration into the social world of the patron. Tilyou once stated that what Americans desired was 'relief in unconsidered muscular action'.[36] His recognition of this need led to a plethora of mechanical amusement rides that had one thing in common – the gimmick of throwing people together in physical and gregarious ways. Steeplechase challenged Victorian conventions and asked people to lay aside their inhibitions. Even a prudish schoolteacher, following a visit to Steeplechase, said that 'when I saw the big crowd here, everyone

George Tilyou's revolutionary funny face.

with the brakes off, the spirit of the place got the better of me'.[37] Machines ranging from the Human Roulette Wheel, the Barrel of Love, the Dew Drop and, not to be forgotten, the Steeplechase, allowed people to bump and grind into one another, to become the objects of a voyeuristic crowd, and allowed couples to meet and interact in erotic ways. One of the park's most famous attractions, the Blow-Hole Theater (later called the Insanitarium), featured clowns who prodded and shocked people. All the while, a seated audience would watch with delight as men were clobbered over the head with props and women's skirts flew up over their waists as a result of blowholes at the exits. As people went through the experience and later exited, they took part in a social rite of passage. Tilyou 'discovered that customers would pay for the privilege of entertaining other customers, that people liked seeing shows, but they liked seeing people more'.[38] Like the popular stunt shows and game shows that are brought to theme parks including Universal Studios, Tilyou made a major advance in his use of real people as the stage on which amusement was built.

The Human Roulette Wheel at Steeplechase Park revolutionized theme parks as spaces of human kinetics.

In 1907, after a massive fire that destroyed the park, ever the showman, Tilyou emblazoned on a sign the famous words, 'To inquiring friends: I have troubles today that I did not have yesterday. I had troubles yesterday that I have not today. On this site will be erected shortly a better, bigger, greater Steeplechase Park. Admission to the burning ruins: 10 cents.' Steeplechase was rebuilt and lasted longer than the other Coney Island parks, finally closing its doors in 1964. Though Tilyou's rivals at Luna Park and Dreamland would surpass his ability to have the grandest and most spectacular attractions and rides, his insights about human desire for entertainment provided an important legacy for the amusement and theme parks that would follow Steeplechase. Steeplechase did not particularly influence the contemporary theme park in terms of theme lands and mood landscapes, but it did establish the important principle of the amusement park as a mechanical response to the body. Without Steeplechase the idea of the amusement park ride being intimately connected to the patron might not have taken hold. Tilyou's park also predates Disney, Universal Studios, Busch Gardens and Six Flags parks in terms of the attention to perceived danger in a safe environment and the sense of a loss of control all the while exerting control. Perhaps the biggest contribution of Steeplechase to the theme park corpus is the idea that in an amusement oasis all contradictions of the outside world can be happily resolved.

After a year at Tilyou's Steeplechase Frederic Thompson and Elmer Dundy took their A Trip to the Moon and opened Luna Park in 1903. It is reported that Thompson and Dundy needed to borrow change for the ticket booths just to open the park. However, it was so popular that the duo turned a profit just six weeks after opening, in part due to the hype that surrounded the opening of a new Coney Island park.[39] Luna took inspiration from the moon itself, not just in its popular attraction A Trip to the Moon, but in the sense that it was conceived as a 'radiant reflection of energy, never the same or in the same place from one moment to the next'.[40] The site of Luna was the razed Sea Lion Park of Paul Boyton; only the popular Shoot-the-Chutes water ride was spared in the razing. More than any of the other early amusement parks at Coney Island, Luna Park reflects the greatest historical resonances of the contemporary theme park. Unlike Steeplechase's emphasis on mechanical amusement rides, Luna creates another world – a theme – through architecture and technologies of illusion. Photographs, postcards and accounts from the day attest to the wonder that Luna created; as one visitor said 'Ah, God, What might the prophet have written in Revelations if only he had first beheld a spectacle like this?' Luna was the first fantasy setting within the space of an amusement park. It was, according to some, first conceived as 'another world's fair, but before long they realized it was something better', something more.[41] Luna was the brainchild of two innovative practitioners, the disgruntled architect Fred Thompson and the showman and promoter Elmer Skip Dundy. Dundy was in part encouraged to go into show business following frequent visits of Buffalo Bill Cody to his home and Thompson is remembered for his early struggles with finding his identity as an architect.[42]

Entering Luna Park, the visitor was immediately struck with the visual scale of the park and how it offered a collection of incredible sights, attractions and forms of entertainment that were anything but ordinary. As Fred Thompson opined, 'When a stranger arrives at Coney Island . . . the first thing that impresses him is change – difference. His eyes tell him that he is in a different world – a dream world, perhaps a nightmare world – where all is bizarre and fantastic – crazier than the craziest part of Paris –

gayer and more different from the everyday world.'[43] In this sense Luna was larger and more spectacular than Steeplechase. It had more rides, more spectacular attractions and shows, incredible displays of electricity and forms of constant amusement and performance that created the sense of the 'other world' that today's theme parks demonstrate. What made this otherworldliness possible was architecture, and this is no surprise given Fred Thompson's significant yet troubled background in the profession. Thompson struggled to rebel against the Beaux-Arts tradition, and eventually he found professional success in copying and reauthenticating buildings like the Moorish palace he created at the 1898 Trans-Mississippi and International Exposition in Omaha. The building won Thompson a prize, and though he had no knowledge of African-Moorish culture, he demonstrated a sense of an 'architecture for speed-reading' or an ability to conceive of readily understandable and consumable architectural structures (now common to the world of the theme park and the Las Vegas Strip).[44] Such symbolic architecture would become the norm at Luna and Coney Island, and it seemed that Thompson had perfected a commercial architectural style that helped 'advertise what was "on sale" inside and the color of its contents as effectively as a billboard'.[45] Thompson made architecture consumable for the masses at the amusement park, and Dundy helped him sell it.

Like the world's fairs before it Luna established the normalcy of the abundance of multiple design styles and geographic referents in one space, but it went beyond that. Castle turrets, Dutch windmills, Roman chariots, sculptures of animals, Japanese gardens, giant building blocks and Oriental features peacefully coexisted in a 'system of metaphorical meaning', according to architect Rem Koolhaas.[46] The architectural eclecticism of Luna Park had never been seen before in any amusement park. Before the Bellagio in

Las Vegas, Luna Park emphasized luxury through its architecture, and before the Circus Circus and Excalibur, it demonstrated the powerful and playful role that architecture can have in people's lives. Beyond the buildings, signs and exterior features, Luna also included numerous rides that bespoke of the effort to create worlds within a world – the canals of Venice, the naval spectacular War of the Worlds, the floods of Galveston and Jonestown spectaculars and the popular reality-based drama Fire and Flames. Much like a television set with multiple channels, Luna's fantasy vistas created places of a wide variety and origin that could all be seen in the span of one day.

As one critic said of Coney Island at the time, 'the very architecture roars at you',[47] and Luna Park proved that architecture could perform. Thompson himself said that he wanted 'no definite style of architecture' at Luna Park, and he deliberately eschewed straight lines and anything reminiscent of the Beaux-Arts tradition.[48] Luna's architect also understood that building and facade was not enough to create an illusionary oasis for customers. Thompson and Dundy added 250,000 incandescent lights to dot the minarets of the park, and they kept the prominent Shoot-the-Chutes ride from the park on which Luna was built. By having the Shoot-the-Chutes in the park's centre they guaranteed a geographical primacy of vision in which the centre of the park radiated out to the other sights and attractions. This design is of particular importance in later theme parks, like Epcot with its dramatic World Showcase in which pavilions surround a prominent water feature and the Lost Kennywood section of Kennywood park that pays homage to earlier such uses of water rides. Luna also included an impressive electric tower that became an instant symbol of the park and later influenced the development of observation tower rides at many amusement and theme parks. The tower must

have been especially spectacular as it gave people the power of viewing from above and down on the others inside the park – a radical and simultaneous reformulation of sociality and vision.

In addition to eclectic architecture that performed for its customers, Luna Park included an array of rides, amusements and concessions that had never before been assembled in an amusement park. Theatre acts, ballrooms, casinos, performative spectacles of trapeze acts and people being shot out of cannons, animal shows and circuses, elephant rides and mechanical rides that rivalled those of Steeplechase, all existed in spontaneous and cacophonous juxtaposition. Were it not an amusement space, these elements would likely not be tolerated together. This speaks of the emergence of 'amusement world picture' that would rival

Spectacular architecture at Luna Park, early 20th century, which at the time represented a previously unprecedented sight in the amusement park.

the realities of other 'world pictures', like cinema, literature and theatre. Whereas some features of the world's fair were austere – almost museum-like in their displays – Luna Park featured raucous entertainment that was ever-changing, and its overall spectacle was one for all of the senses. The overarching principle of these features is summed up in Thompson's advice that Luna was about 'movement, movement, movement everywhere'.[49] In Thompson's mind, the eye as it gazed at Luna's architecture should not be static, and neither should the amusements, shows and moving rides that made up the park's landscape. Above all, as these elements combined, an order of synaesthetic potential was created.

Movement and architectural performance created the greatest spectacle of the amusement park, often in ways that had been previously unimagined. The value of spectacle was fully established

The prominence of Luna Park's Shoot-the-Chutes provided a centre that later theme parks would similarly utilize.

through Thompson's amusement principles. He regularly featured elephants that dived down their own Shoot-the-Chute rides, and he famously filmed the public electrocution of Topsy the elephant after the animal failed to die after ingesting poisoned carrots. Mount Vesuvius would sporadically erupt throughout the day at Luna, and its pyrotechnic show guaranteed that there would never be a dull moment inside the fabricated oasis of Luna Park. Like the public fire and water shows of Las Vegas's Mirage and Bellagio today, Thompson and Dundy realized the need to

An aerial swing at Luna Park helped guide the theme park as a conveyor of movement as a form of pleasure.

constantly stupefy the patron. Thompson once wrote of his amusement philosophy that when people visit Coney Island 'they are not in a serious mood . . . They have enough seriousness in their every-day lives, and the keynote of the thing they do demand is change. Everything must be different from ordinary experience. What is presented to them must have life, action, motion, sensation, surprise, shock, swiftness or else comedy.'[50] Like the idea of the *Gesamtkunstwerk*, the total, integrated and complete artwork, Thompson's entertainment philosophy was unflinchingly focused on a maximalist approach.

Luna also proved that the theme park could be a franchise. In one year alone, Luna Park saw 4 million people enter its gates – a number that would be impressive even for a contemporary amusement park. Following the success of Coney Island's Luna, many other Luna parks (all illegitimate) began to appear in other parts of the world, including Melbourne, Rome, Berlin and Buenos Aires, as well as in five American cities.[51] By 1912 Luna was in bankruptcy,

The great naval battle spectacle 'The Monitor and the Merrimac' brought historical recreations unavailable in other media to the amusement park.

and Thompson, unable to operate it effectively after the death of Dundy, and struggling with alcohol, was never able to regain the glory of the park. Though Luna attempted to revitalize itself into the 1940s, it closed forever in 1944. In many respects it affected the contemporary theme park form: it offered unbelievable architecture and combined it in a fantasy world – a 'themed park' – for its patrons; it showed that variety entertainment that was constantly changing was to be the norm of the theme park; and it showed that the customer must be constantly put in the midst of the amusement drama. With the architect once writing that he sought the 'pure and good' of the public, Thompson's Luna Park also reflected a future trend of the uncontaminated, safe, clean and happy theme park.[52]

The last of Coney Island's major amusement parks, Dreamland, was the island's most expensive and lavish park and yet, ironically, the worst received by the amusement public. Dreamland opened in 1904, the product of former Republican state senator and real estate tycoon William Reynolds. Like Walt Disney later, Reynolds understood the need to have a large property on which to build his park, and he shrewdly negotiated deals with the city for his land. At a cost of over 2 million dollars – three times the cost of Luna Park – Dreamland was easily the most excessive and extravagant of the Coney parks.[53] Casting aside the experimental and postmodern architectural eclecticism of Luna Park, Reynolds opted for an austere, sober and snobbish white colour as well as numerous allusions to the Beaux-Arts traditions made famous at the World's Columbian Exposition of 1893. Visitors were taken with the level of detail given to Dreamland's architecture and attractions. Most amazing of all were the lights – a visual feast that one playwright of the time described as 'a thing never to be forgotten'.[54] One million lights flickered along the park's buildings and atop the massive Beacon Tower, which beamed a light 50 miles out to sea,

much like the powerful light that now adorns the top of the Luxor Las Vegas pyramid.

With architecture and moralistic fantasies Reynolds sought to reverse the bacchanalia that were common in the other amusement parks of Coney Island. In short, he attempted to create high art in the people's empire. The first attention that Reynolds gave to his amusement park was to establish everything on a bigger, grander and more lavish scale than his competitors. Like the casino wars that have consumed the Las Vegas Strip – in which millions of dollars are spent on new, competitor casinos – Reynolds created a scenario in which capitalism was the driving force of the amusement park.

A typical scene in Luna Park, at the time as idyllic as any journey to nature sites.

The attention of Tilyou to human kinetics and desires at Steeplechase and the emphasis of Thompson and Dundy on creating a fantasy oasis for customers were both rejected in favour of offering a pleasure refuge that was based on the principle of capital accumulation and the commodity. Like the forms of copying that are now common to consumer society – including illegal MP3 downloads, pirated software and movies – Reynolds used his money and political might to steal six attractions from Luna Park, including a famous infant incubator attraction run by the world-famous Doctor Couney. Dreamland had a tower, but it was bigger than Luna's, and it had a Shoot-the-Chutes, but it was more powerful and higher than Luna's. Many of the park's other attractions, including historical recreation rides and spectacular pyrotechnic demonstrations, were

Dreamland's tower by night.

Many years later, the Luxor's beam, Las Vegas.

lifted and copied from Luna Park. Like the roller coaster war that sometimes plagues the contemporary amusement industry, the efforts of Reynolds to secure the biggest and the 'best' at his park did not necessarily result in patron satisfaction.

At the same time amusement parks like Dreamland were beginning to tap into the public's consciousness. Written in 1909, the song 'Meet Me To-Night in Dreamland' reflected the vast popular appeal of the amusement park. Its words spoke of a sense of the idyllic, and of the sublime: 'Dreaming of you, that's all I do . . . meet me in the land of dreams. Meet me tonight in Dreamland, under the silv'ry moon . . . There let my dreams come true.' What songs like these reflect is the growing willingness of the population to be satisfied by commercial amusements. In the machine age of the amusement park that would follow through the 1920s even greater emphasis was placed on the idea of fusing human desires with mechanical and simulated technologies of entertainment. In more ways than one the machine and the garden are harmonized at parks like Dreamland. Like Luna, but again on a

View of Dreamland, 1907.

larger scale, Dreamland offered lavish spectacles, like a show that featured 600 veterans of the Boer War who reenacted their battles in a stadium that seated 12,000. To counter Luna's Fire and Flames, Dreamland offered Fighting the Flames – a much bigger version of the fire spectacular with many more performers than Luna's. Simulation rides also abounded, including gondolas that took people through the canals of Venice, a Haunted Swing that featured *trompe l'oeil* and a Swiss Alps ride that included the sensory effects of refrigerated air on the bodies of riders. The park also included a number of impressively themed attractions, such as an Orient section with gardens, temples and a re-creation of the destruction of Babylon.[55]

Entrance to Creation (Dreamland).

Dreamland represented the first proto-theme park to incorporate active moral instruction and pedagogy as a part of its amusements. Like the white architecture of the park, the attractions prompted a moralistic tone that was a first for Coney Island. Creation featured a biblical tale that included the Garden of Eden and Adam and Eve, while End of the World offered an unapologetic missive for potential sinners among the crowds, and Hell Gate featured a woman being dragged down to the depths of hell, all examples of an eschatology that was entirely new for the theme park. Dreamland's managers often 'touted the educational and scientific nature of their shows'[56] and it is clear that the park takes some of its influence from the technological and commercial wizardry of the world exposition tradition. But, unlike the fairs, many of the 'marvels' on display at Dreamland reflected at best a technology of the useless. One case in point was the park's Leap-Frog Railway, which consisted of two train cars that leapt over each other like frogs but which went nowhere. More like the world's fair, Dreamland incorporated a major ethnological tradition under the supervision of Samuel Gumpertz, who would later become the park's manager. Gumpertz put on display people from all over the world – some of whom he smuggled illegally into the United States – including fifty Igorots from the Philippines and an entire Inuit village. Dreamland also included a 'Midget City' whose performers lived on the premises inside a reproduction of fifteenth-century Nuremberg.

The park set an important tradition, namely the first effort to actively control the flow and pacing of patrons at the park. The design of park walkways alternated between level and inclined patterns, assuring that everyone could have a view of the park's vistas, and other design elements emphasized the control of massive crowds, especially to reduce congestion.[57] Though it handled such control effectively, Dreamland may have failed at the psychological and affective levels. One park operator commented that 'We sought to appeal to a highly developed sense of the artistic, but it did not take us long to discover that Coney Island was scarcely the place for that sort of thing. Architectural and decorative beauty were virtually lost upon the great majority of visitors.'[58]

Like the otherworldly experience of religion, Dreamland promoted an approach to amusement that would resume with the efforts of Walt Disney in the 1960s and to an even greater degree in biblical theme parks like the Holy Land Experience in Orlando, Florida. For some of Dreamland's guests the emphasis on moral instruction may have resulted in their amusements being 'elevated to an ideological plane', which, in the end, may have been too heavy to handle.[59] In 1911 a devastating fire engulfed Dreamland. In bitter irony, during a worker mishap at the Hell Gate attraction, a fire swelled and consumed the entire park. With the fire, the park spread into mass chaos: premature babies in the infant incubator exhibition, though initially feared to have burned, were saved, but many of the animals were not so lucky. One lion attempting to escape the fire was described as having a burning mane and 'sparks trailing "like torrents from its tail"' prior to it being shot at by policemen and finally killed with an axe.[60] Following the fire William Reynolds decided not to rebuild Dreamland. Though it never gained the popularity of Luna or Steeplechase, Dreamland left noticeable traces, perhaps ones that have allowed unfavourable trends to surface in the contemporary

Fire brings destruction to Dreamland.

theme park, including forms of entertainment that focus not on the patron but on the producer. Reynolds's capitalist approach to the proto-theme park is perhaps the greatest of these influences to be seen in the present. The attempt to moralize and educate the public within an amusement space also established a trend that is still seen in today's theme parks.

As one documentary on Coney Island offered,

> in the end, the world that Coney Island ushered in overtook it. The towers of Luna Park were just as tall and just as bright, but Manhattan's grew taller and eventually outshone them. Coney's mechanical diversions were being superseded by the automobile. Immigrant parents who had saved up all year to spend one day at Coney grew old. Many of their children prospered and moved to the suburbs.[61]

The traditions that the amusement parks established – including enclosed amusement spaces, themed attractions, dramatic re-creations and forms of simulation, spectacular rides and incredible performances and shows – seemed to fade away as public amusements changed in tandem with society. The dream to push society in new directions through public amusements took a hiatus. Not until the 1920s, with the boom of a new amusement park tradition, would this dream continue, and not until the 1960s, with the theme park revolution, would it be realized.

2 Theme Park as Land

> A sense of place is, perhaps, the ultimate synthesis, the bringing
> together of all dimensions of environment, perception and experience
> into a vast whole.
> Stephen F. Mills[1]

The craving for a sense of place is at the heart of the contemporary theme park. As the theme park's primogenitor, the early amusement park of Coney Island offered fantastical landscapes that made forms of conceptual travel possible. Visitors to Sea Lion Park could ride the Shoot-the-Chutes and replicate a wild water adventure, those at Steeplechase could understand what it was like to be a jockey atop a racehorse, patrons at Luna Park could experience out-of-this-world travel on the Trip to the Moon ride, while patrons of Dreamland could be transported to the gates of Hell and then safely return to their normal lives. What each of the early Coney Island parks offered was conceptual travel. A visitor from Manhattan could travel just a short distance to experience pleasures and sights that had normally been possible only on the Grand Tour. As cinema began to emerge there was competition between these two forms, but amusement parks challenged even the conceptual travel of the cinema by claiming an attachment to physicality and sociality – one could partake in experiences while feeling them personally and being around others at the same time. The powerful combination of bodily and social entertainments made the amusement parks' conceptual travel a truly unique form of amusement.

The early amusement parks of Coney Island offered geographic, architectural and performative approaches that characterized

them as quasi-theme parks. They displayed elements that would eventually be deployed in contemporary theme parks, but they lacked the coherence of vision that would lead to the contemporary theme park's success as well as its controversy. Like cinema, theatre, vaudeville and video games, theme parks project an otherworldliness. They allow people to conceptually travel to other places and other time periods, resulting in sensory and mood orientations that contrast with those of everyday life. The power of the otherworldly, especially as founded in religion, is exactly the ability of a force to transport an individual – physically, mentally, aesthetically, politically and existentially – to some other place and some other state of being. As the individual is transported she forgets where she once was and instead reorients to the new place. Architectural studies of the early cathedrals indicate that architecture played a major role in religion's creation of the otherworldly. Especially as the senses were used in combination with architecture, the senses helped 'clarify the structure and substance of the entire building, revealing its essential character'.[2] Though theme parks are generally not religious sites, they share

Atlantis: The Sunken City at Steeplechase Park was one example of the emergence of fantasy worlds within the space of the amusement park.

characteristics with the medieval cathedral, especially as they use architecture, geography and modes of performance to reference all of the senses for the ends of amusement. Theme parks give themselves a place by being spaces of hypersensation. Unlike religion, which adds to its power due to its embedded social status, early amusement parks lacked the social capital to make a meaningful impact on people's lives. What they needed was a theme.

Parc Astérix, located in Paris, France, is an interesting contemporary theme park. Parc Astérix uses myth as a means of thematically organizing its rides, attractions and shows. Patrons may view a historical portrayal of eighteenth-century French mousquetaires, and are given the kinetic ride Tonnerre de Zeus. A Gaul village, a Parisian boulevard area with classic street performers and the Les Artisans dans la Rue de Paris, which features potters, glassblowers and other craftspeople practising their simulated trades, complete the theming of the park. Theming 'involves the use of an overarching theme, such as western, to create a holistic and integrated spatial organization of a consumer venue' and theming represents

Universal's Islands of Adventure.

the movement of the amusement park form to the theme park form.[3] Early amusement parks like Luna and Dreamland offered varied otherworldly attractions that in themselves were themed, but there was no overarching theme given to large units within the park's space (theme lands) nor to the entire park itself. Parc Astérix shows that it is possible and profitable to attach a major concept, the myth, to the landscape of the theme park. This effort – to theme the amusement park – gives the amusement form the narrative that it will need to become fully significant. As Terence Young has considered, 'a theme park's landscape gives form and narrative to a myth, but it also gives it a place'.[4] Parc Astérix utilizes two significant associations – the first the popular French cartoon character Astérix, the second the powerful role of religious myth, including that of Roman and Greek origins. Parc Astérix emphasizes that providing an amusement park with a theme may exploit the already vivid cultural associations present in people's minds. It can act through architecture more effectively when it has acted on culture.

The contemporary theme park takes the early amusement park's enclosure – the separation of the amusement space from the rest of the world, which occurred first at Sea Lion Park – and embellishes it. It is not enough to merely separate itself from the outside world – for even shopping malls do that – instead it gives itself a sense of place that will seem natural, as if a climatic zone. Even in the presence of its artificial architecture, symbolism and cultural references, theming offers a naturalness. As one member of a theming design company offered, 'Our guests don't know what it is about these places that makes them so engaging – yet they find them very compelling.'[5] As many failed theme parks, including Freedomland, prove, the balance between the corporeal and experiential joys of the unthemed amusement park and the cognitive

and aesthetic foci of the theme park is an extremely delicate one. In order for the theme park to complete its journey away from the amusement park and to effect the right amusement balance it must attend to two significant details.

First, the amusement park must find a spatial and architectural form that will resonate with people. Simply having a grand theme, as Dreamland's moralism illustrated, will not necessarily interest the patron. For it to become a theme park, the amusement park needs an architecture of persuasion that will convince patrons to 'crave imagined locales more than . . . actual ones'.[6] At venues like Epcot in Orlando and its World Showcase, visitors commonly express how they are able to see multiple world places and cultures

The massive statue of the god Zeus at the Tonnerre de Zeus, Parc Astérix.

in one place: 'this is the only place where you can actually sample different lifestyles . . . together', while others say, 'you get to go to all the countries in one day, in twenty-four hours you see everything . . . it's great, and then just move right on to the next country; they change accents as you go'.[7] Theming operates through multiple architectural, cognitive, cultural, performative and aesthetic levels, and primary to theming is the concept of a delivery device through which to project the theming of a particular locale. In the pleasure gardens of Europe the delivery device was mainly visual and topographic – the eye and the garden coincided to produce pleasure and entertainment – while in the world's fair tradition the device is sensorial and consumerist. In the contemporary theme park these earlier efforts to naturalize the space of consumption are realized in four approaches to an architecture of persuasion: place (real and imagined), events and time periods, moods and people and cultures. The particular means by which the theme park approaches its spatial and architectural decisions is not

The Venetian Gardens at Coney Island: the movement of foreign space and culture into the domestic space of the amusement park.

as significant, though, as the way in which it fills in the gaps that may develop as a person moves from ride to attraction and from theme land to theme land within the theme park.

The amusement parks of Coney Island proved that lavish architecture could be successfully used as an amusement delivery device. Even in cases in which one might think that the architecture is too outlandish, it is used in remarkably successful ways to connect with the amusement park patron. But what occurs when amusement park architecture begins to saturate social and cultural spaces? Would people grow tired of such architecture, perhaps as some have of the quasi-theme park space of the Las Vegas Strip? As much as the architecture of persuasion could be successful in a material sense it lacked the social capital that gives religious structures like the cathedral unquestioned status. And it also lacked the ability to silence critics who claim that the theme park is mere artifice and inconsequential consumerism. What it needs – to go along with its first requirement of a meaningful spatial and architectural form – is an ability to fill in the space between its conceptual bricks. It needs an architecture of juxtapositions, one that will prove to the world that the combinations and assemblages of symbols, cultural references and sensory orders are legitimate.

One of the post-Coney Island influences on the development of themed amusement parks was the 1939–40 New York World's Fair. The fair was divided into seven distinctive zones that projected a form similar to the theme land of the contemporary theme park. Zones included amusement, medicine and public health, food, community interests, production and distribution, and others. Like earlier world's fairs the 1939–40 Fair reflected a museum-like concern with displaying objects, people, technology and re-created places in distinctive categories. The 'exhibitionary complex' of the world's fair allowed previously disconnected categories – like amusement, industry, ethnology and technology – to come together in an uncanny combination of place and form. As Tony Bennett offers, this complex 'involved . . . the transfer of objects and bodies from the enclosed and private domains in which they had been previously displayed . . . into progressively more open and public arenas'.[8] At the centre of the complex was the wonder of the fair patron who walked in the themed landscapes, gazed upon commodities and used theming as an opportunity to reflect on self, other and world.

The world's fair offers the patron experiences similar to the *Wunderkammer* – the cabinet of curiosities. What is most important in the *Wunderkammer* is the reduction of the tension between that which is represented – the pastiche of things in the room of display – and the person who visually receives and cognitively interprets the representation. The viewer must be persuaded to accept what is given, even when it seems to be artificial, haphazard or crazy. The 1939–40 World's Fair took the principle of the *Wunderkammer* and used it to ease the tensions between the artificiality of goods and modes of consumption and the times, places, cultures and moods it presented to people. Unlike previous fairs, the 1939–40 version made explicit reference to its artifice: it detailed why each 'highly important phase of modern life' was represented, it justified the specific material elements of the fair – architecture, sculpture, murals, landscaping, colour and lighting – and it broke from previous fairs in offering the 'zone' as a form of escape.[9] As the fair's guidebook rationalized, 'This development enables the visitor to escape, for the first time, much of the mental confusion and the physical exhaustion which have invariably hindered his previous attempts to see and understand a great exposition.'[10] Unlike the raucous Midway Plaisance of the 1893 Exposition, the visitor would become the centre of the 1939–40 Fair, soothed into the artificial landscape and told how to accept an assemblage of the uncanny and the impossible.

The 1939–40 Fair also replaced the midway – a singular strip of land that it declared to be 'old-fashioned' – with a loop, much like the contemporary loop of a theme park in which the patron goes round and round in the amusement cycle.[11] It was in this circular loop of amusement that the fair gave itself to the theme park. It offered a juxtaposition of amusements that, like the *Wunderkammer*, made no sense on the surface. Here Admiral Byrd's Penguin Island mated with a re-creation of mythical Amazonian women, an archery range of women in Robin Hood suits with the military-themed Camp George Washington, a Cuban village complete with food, fiestas and costumes (but no high culture) paired with the crime-themed Gang Busters, a Blarney stone and castle ('a real bit of Old Ireland is brought to the Fair') married with a 'faithful reproduction' of Merrie England complete with abridged reproductions of Shakespearian plays, the Gay Nineties of reconstructed old New York dated Salvador Dali's Living Pictures, and villagers wrestle alligators in an 'authentic reproduction' of a Seminole village coalesced with Victoria Falls' references to Africa, nature and landscape. In this moment of the amusement zone of the 1939–40 World's Fair the theme park is given the important architecture of juxtapositions that it will need to complete its vision of the world.[12]

The 1939–40 World's Fair proved that it is possible to connect disparate amusements – whether rides, shows, historical displays, demonstrations or cultural reconstructions – in one space. The amusement parks of Coney Island also illustrated how such an arrangement – a sort of three-dimensional, moving, multi-sensory cabinet of curiosities – was possible. The contemporary theme

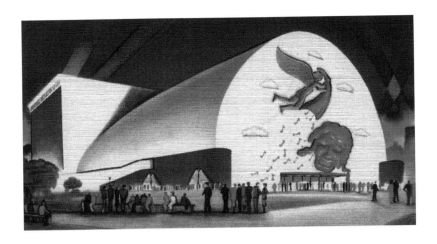

park, whether through referencing place, time and event, mood, or people and culture, makes the radical juxtapositions of architecture and geography complete. As will be illustrated in chapter Four, the seams between places within the landscape of the theme park will need further attention for them to appear natural, to be seamless, especially through the story. With its use of both an affective spatial and architectural form and an assemblage of juxtaposed elements, the theme park is ready to make its appearance.

Unquestionably, the most famous of all theme parks is Disneyland. Opened in 1955 by the famed animator and media mogul Walt Disney, this new concept of park would create a standard for the theme park that would last beyond the twentieth century and would impact parks outside the United States. Significant foundations that Disneyland established included the concept of safe, fun and clean entertainment; the development of abstract theme lands that referenced places, moods or events from the life of Walt Disney; the development of a branded and cross-promotional entertainment platform that would take the theme park out

The music hall at the 1939 World's Fair.

of the theme park; the establishment of a theme park empire that would include parks in Florida, Paris, Tokyo and Hong Kong, as well as a cruise line and private island and smaller locales known as DisneyQuest; the development of high technological approaches, most notably audio-animatronics; the drawing in of corporate sponsors for theme park rides and attractions; the creation of the theme park as a primary tourist destination; the privileging of the family as the basic unit of the park (not the couple, as had been the case at Coney Island); the development of elaborate park transportation systems, including the monorail and people mover systems; the pioneering of new modes of pedestrian control, including Omnimover or continuous loader system rides (Haunted Mansion); and the development of rides that were complete attractions in and of themselves.

One of the most significant advancements of the theme park form is the development of theming – the overarching design given to the various rides, attractions and spaces within the theme park. 'Disneyland subordinated the identities of individual rides, exhibits, and other features to the larger, thematically coordinated environment.'[13] Like Dreamland and other Coney Island amusement parks, Disneyland featured a prominent entrance that would become a hallmark for future theme parks, particularly the Six Flags theme parks. Main Street USA was the theme land that greeted patrons when they entered Disneyland. Walt Disney once said that 'For those of us who remember the carefree time it recreates, Main Street will bring back happy memories. For younger visitors, it is an adventure in turning back the calendar to the days of their grandfather's youth.' Walt Disney's childhood sense of place, derived from Marceline, Missouri, was used to create an ideal Main Street for Disneyland and subsequent Disney theme parks; ironically, Disney's main street would impact the planning of future 'main streets' in small towns across the United States.[14] A second theme land was Adventureland, which included the park's famous Jungle Cruise ride and which reflected Walt Disney's exotic ideal of 'ourselves far from civilization, in the remote jungles of Asia and Africa'. A third land, Frontierland, offered Disney's desire to reconnect people with the frontier past and all of its senses of adventure and 'pioneering spirit'. Fantasyland, a general haven for the childlike, was a themed area that included attractions like Dumbo, Alice in Wonderland and Mr Toad's Wild Ride. Tomorrowland was the theme land that most closely resembled the forward-looking, technological and utopian spirit of the world's fairs. Its spaces included futuristic rides like the popular Space Mountain indoor roller coaster. Later, Walt Disney helped supervise the addition of theme land New Orleans Square, which would later posthumously include the highly popular Haunted Mansion and Pirates of the Caribbean rides.

One of the most important aspects of Disneyland's creation of theme lands is the use of narrative as a means of theming. As an

A view of a typical main street, soon to be exploited at Disney and other theme parks worldwide.

Imagineer once stated, 'at Disney theme parks, a building is not just a building'.[15] Instead, buildings take on the position of story-tellers and 'the obvious function of a building is secondary to its primary purpose: to help tell the story. Each building's foundation not only supports a physical structure, but it also supports a story structure.'[16] Disneyland's use of architecture to tell a story would create a legacy for the theme park industry; subsequent theme parks, often with less capital and creativity, succumbed to the pressure to use the stories created by architectural facades to theme their parks. One of the monumental ways in which Disneyland established a new theming precedent for the theme park is its creation of abstract and more 'perfect' versions of real landscapes and geographies. As previously discussed, Walt's hometown main street would inspire the Main Street section of the park. While visiting Switzerland, Disney's sighting of the real Matterhorn became the inspiration for the faux Matterhorn moun-tain at the park's Matterhorn Bobsleds. Walt's fascination with the railroad and America – in part inspired by the 1948 Chicago Railroad Fair – led to the creation of the Disneyland Railroad.[17] Other more generalized influences on Disneyland included Children's Fairyland, a small amusement park in Oakland, California, which was visited frequently by Walt Disney. Opened in 1950 and consisting of a storybook-themed amusement area, the small park is sometimes considered to be the first theme park in the United States. Fantasy architecture buildings contained stories like Alice in Wonderland, Pinocchio and the Three Little Pigs. Perhaps what compelled Walt Disney the most was the small park's use of a clear story to entertain children and their parents. As Disney would pioneer at his park, a ride should not simply be a visceral pleasure (as it was at Steeplechase Park), it should be a self-contained themed world and a narrative delivery device.

Perhaps the most famous and universally recognizable theme park symbol is the Cinderella Castle. Neuschwanstein Castle of Bavaria, with a number of French castles, inspired Disney to create his perfect iconic castle. Many of Disneyland's attractions, including Cinderella Castle, are engineered down to the most minute details. The attention to detail at Disney, what could be called 'microtheming', would influence later theme parks and quasi-theme parks like those of Las Vegas. The focus on the specifics of them-

Neuschwanstein Castle at Schwangau, Bavaria, Germany, an icon used and recast by Disney.

ing – the nuances of details that might be noticed by a patron in the most obscure and unexpected places – relies on the massive creative agency of Imagineering and a research arm of the theme park. Early in the planning of Disneyland Disney established a research institute (SRI) to analyse the market in which Disneyland would compete. Outdoor fairs, small amusement parks, zoos and even the Forest Lawn Memorial Park cemetery in Glendale, California, were visited to assess patron satisfaction, pedestrian flow and other issues.[18]

What is significant about Disneyland's use of place is its abstraction of it. Whereas previous amusement parks referenced specific places in their recreations – like those of Luna and Dreamland – Disneyland establishes a generalized, metaphorical concept of place. As Disney's theme lands and architecture resonate well beyond the confines of the theme park and into general popular culture, simulated places of Disneyland become effects. Main Street is no longer a specific place – Marceline, Missouri, or even Main Street USA in Disneyland – it becomes a placeless place, a place not of the material realm of architecture but of the cognitive one of architectural imagination. Disneyland, it could be argued, was 'less an amusement park than a state of mind'.[19]

In a major embellishment of George Tilyou's earlier efforts to connect with the patron Disney saw the need to associate the theme park experience directly with the lives of his customers, or 'guests' as the dramaturgical term (that Disney also originated) indicates:

To all who come to this happy place – welcome. Disneyland is your land. Here age relives fond memories of the past and here youth may savor the challenge and promise of the future. Disneyland is dedicated to the ideals, the dreams, and the hard facts that have created America . . . with the hope that it will be a source of joy and inspiration to all the world. Thank you.

So reads the dedication given by Walt Disney on the opening of his park in 1955. Most significant in Disney's dedication is his emphasis on Disneyland being *your* land. In contrast with some of the amusement parks with which he was familiar, including those of Coney Island, Walt Disney wanted to establish the theme park as a place that emphasized controlled entertainment, not the raucous type that was popularized in the early amusement parks. Whereas Coney Island aspired to be proletarian and of the masses, Disneyland strove to be a middle-class experience of the family. Disneyland sought to 'dispense with the spatial disorganization, surly attendants, unkempt grounds . . . that reportedly prevailed at conventional amusement parks'.[20] Disneyland does more than establish a profitable geographical and architectural form for the theme park, it also prepares society for it, by attending to domains like population and civility, and it creates a mode of reception for the form. Without Disneyland people would not use the term 'theme park' as commonly and wildly as they often do.

Like Disneyland, Six Flags Over Texas established theming by an attention to place. Opened by oil tycoon Angus G. Wynne, Jr in 1961, Six Flags Over Texas was the first theme park to follow the model of Disney. Six Flags corporate history indicates that Wynne visited Disneyland in the late 1950s and was inspired 'to create a theme park that would be large in scope and filled with fantasy, like Disneyland, yet closer to the Guests so that a family visit would be easier and more affordable. And in the tradition of his wild west Texas roots, Wynne wanted more emphasis on thrills and excitement.'[21] Like Disneyland, Six Flags Over Texas emphasized the subdivision of the entire theme park into theme lands; in this case, more emphasis is given to actual landscapes as forms of inspiration. The six flags that had flown over the state of Texas – Spain, France, Mexico, the Republic of Texas, the Confederacy and

the United States of America – became the vantage points through which the park was themed. The Confederacy was eventually changed to the Old South, and other sections – including one referencing Wynne's background and the park's oil derrick observation tower – were added. Six Flags Over Texas also pioneered a number of new rides, including the log flume, and attempted to use these rides as a way of countering Disney's major theme park capital. Later Six Flags opened parks across the United States, and then in Mexico, Canada and Europe. Whereas Disneyland created theme lands based on more abstract and imaginary locations, Six Flags Over Texas proved that it was possible to theme a park in accord with more traditional geographic associations. It also attempted to do something that Disney could not – combine the thrill ride emphasis of the amusement park with the thematic orientation of the theme park. In this way, along with the other

Disney's California Adventure Park. Within the world of the theme park, clean, sanitized and picturesque spaces combine in one spatial order.

Six Flags parks to follow, Six Flags Over Texas provided a formidable model for the new theme park.

Theming has also been approached through references to the past, including specific historical periods, time periods and associated moods, and even calendrical events. Freedomland was originally billed as the 'Disneyland of the East', and it aimed to educate the public: 'By re-creating the scope of the American adventure, Freedomland brings history to life, makes an educational experience vastly entertaining.'[22] The New York park was opened five years after Disneyland, and in many ways attempted to augment Disneyland's successes in theming. Freedomland took the explicit American experience of Disneyland – such as Frontierland, Main Street and so forth – and subdivided the United States into seven territories, including Little Ole New York (1850–1900), Chicago (1871), The Great Plains (1803–1900), San Francisco (1906), the Old Southwest (1890), New Orleans–Mardi Gras and Satellite City–The Future. Within each of the themed areas Freedomland strategically used theming as a historical form of citation. Unlike Disneyland's generalized, abstract and fantasy-based representations of the United States, Freedomland illustrated that theme parks could utilize more specific referents in their creation of themed landscapes. The New York section represented the region with horse-drawn streetcars, an old-fashioned ice cream shop, a traditional brewery and a political pep rally show that emphasized bands, political speeches and a recreation of a New York bank robbery. Chicago emphasized the infamous Great Chicago Fire of 1871, similar in scope to Fire and Flames and Fighting the Flames of Luna and Dreamland, but without the major cast of actors. The region also focused on Native Americans in ways reminiscent of the ethnological exoticism of the world's fairs. The Great Plains evoked the past through stagecoaches, army stockades and a number of

Borden's branded exhibits, including a working farm. San Francisco referenced the fur trade in a boat ride that looked similar to Disney's Jungle Cruise, harbour seals, a Chinese restaurant and a dark ride that recreated the devastating earthquake that hit the city in 1906. The Old Southwest section offered mining attractions, rides on real burros, Mexican restaurants and singing revues. New Orleans included the interesting horse-drawn wagon ride Civil War, which ended with the passengers finding themselves in the middle of a re-created battle. The section also had a pirate adventure similar to Disney's Pirates of the Caribbean ride and a tornado simulation ride. Satellite City resembled the futuristic focus of the world's fairs, including the one of 1939. The area, like Disneyland's Tomorrowland, gave visitors a sense of the 'future', complete with new-age automobiles and trips into outer space.

Freedomland was not a success. It closed just four years after it was completed, and its history is rife with stories of accidents, armed robberies, a disgruntled public, competition from the 1964–5 New York World's Fair and a lack of company vision. The park experimented briefly with altering its historical and pedagogical focus by revamping the theme lands, laying off many of the park's roaming, themed performers and adding more thrill rides.[23] However, Freedomland was an interesting experiment in theming. Its emphasis on specific historical periods, more geographical specificity and attractions that closely fit the area being themed all offer a glimpse of theming that seems unfamiliar today. Its sense of nostalgia and its development of an approach that emphasized that historical periods and specific geographical locations could be represented by key symbols would come to influence later theme parks, including Busch Gardens, and quasi-theme parks, like the New York–New York Hotel and Casino. Unfortunately, these points are lost on critics and members of the public who point to the failures of Freedomland.[24]

Like Freedomland, a number of China's theme parks model space on the real spaces of the world, ranging from the major landmarks of nations and the wonders of natural landscape to famous cultural and consumer districts. Beijing Happy Valley may prove to be one of China's most successful theme parks. Like the model of thematic land established by Disney, this park organizes space based on six theme lands: Firth Forest, Atlantis, Aegean Sea, Lost Maya, Shangri-La and Ant Kingdom. Unlike Freedomland's referencing of actual places and historical events from the United States, Happy Valley uses mystical associations of theming, including the past civilizations of the Maya and the Greeks and the fictional world of Shangri-La. Perhaps this form of landscape is more appropriate for the customer who wishes to escape the harshness of everyday life – the American Civil War certainly seems more conceptually messy than Shangri-La.

A unique trend in Chinese theme parks is the emphasis on recreations of actual places of the world, but typically in miniature form. At Window of the World in Shenzhen visitors find

The Civil War ride at Freedomland in which patrons were asked to live through the American Civil War on a theme park ride.

miniature versions of the world's great landmarks: the Eiffel Tower, Stonehenge, the British Houses of Parliament, the Taj Mahal, Mount Fuji, Versailles, the pyramids of Egypt, the White House, the temples of Babylon, the New York City skyline and many others. With each 'window of the world', visitors may take part in themed activities that connect to the given place – camel riding outside the miniaturized pyramids of Egypt or eating Mexican food near the replicas of famous Mexican architecture. Like the similar theme park in Taiwan known as Window on China, theme parks of this sort suggest the motto, 'Shrinking the Globe to Magnify the Thrills'.[25]

Splendid China, also located in Shenzhen, similarly uses miniature models of the world – though in this case focused exclusively on China – as a means of compressing travel into one location. A sister park of the same name closed in Orlando, Florida, in part due to protests by Buddhist monks and political activists who took issue with the park's depictions of Tibet's Potala Palace and representations of ethnic minorities and suggestions that these representations legitimated China's occupation of Tibet. Responding to such claims in the 1990s a park manager said bluntly, 'We're a theme park. Nothing more.'[26] While the manager dismissed any sort of politicizing of the park, it is clear that in the new global age theme parks play a vital part in the politics of world cultures. Even more than many theme parks in the United States and Europe, Chinese theme parks feature spectacular shows and entertainment that like approaches of architecture suggest an authenticity of form. The Chinese Ethnic Culture Park pays homage to numerous ethnic minorities of China and their associated architecture. The park offers customers an escape from the harsh urban environment of the outside world and supplants it with a world of harmony, lush vegetation and calming performances.[27]

Chinese theme parks, spurred by the spread of Western-style capitalism and consumerism, reflect a diversity of themes, entertainment styles and service approaches that rival those of any other nation in the world: from Shanghai Wild Animal Park in Shanghai, to the military-themed Minsk World in Shenzhen, to Egyptian, space, Weimar and Swiss-themed venues in many other parts of the country. What the Chinese theme park illustrates more vividly than other nations' parks is the ability to develop niche or boutique theme parks that are responses to new trends in culture. Space-themed parks, for example, reflect China's growing emergence in the space race, telecommunications and technology. While critics frequently dismiss all theme parks as forms of fancy, China's amusement traditions illustrate how theme parks are interesting measures of the culture from which they draw their attractions.

Theming is an approach to entertainment and consumerism that utilizes multiple representational modes. Holiday World in Santa Claus, Indiana, opened in 1946 under the name Santa Claus Land. The park is argued to be the first theme park – an honour contested by Knott's Berry Farm and Disneyland.[28] Its theme lands

In numerous theme parks, the world is represented in miniature form, as is the case at Window on China in Taiwan. Here, even the most commonplace symbols and brands become magical.

include ones based on the calendar and on specific holiday occasions: Halloween, Christmas, Fourth of July and Thanksgiving (added in 2006). The park's Christmas section takes the idea of Christmas and makes it an everyday, if not less symbolic, event. Children can talk to Santa Claus year round and gaze up at a large Christmas tree. Halloween extends the theming of the park to a number of attractions, including an Edgar Allan Poe-inspired 'Raven' roller coaster, a Legend of Sleepy Hollow ride, and the HallowSwings, which reference the park's Halloween theme and feature a flying carousel ride complete with bat sculptures and childlike images of vampires and ghosts. Within the Fourth of July section are loose references to American Independence, including Paul Revere's Midnight Ride, a Freedom Train and country and gospel performances. Thanksgiving includes a Plymouth Rock Cafe, a turkey-themed troika and the Gobbler Getaway, in which riders go 'through the town of Autumn Falls and try to help turkey farmer Cornelius Van Snoodle locate his missing flock'.[29] The many themed attractions of Holiday World are interesting in that they

Window of the World, Shenzhen, China.

indirectly reference their subjects – the holidays – and do so in a way that heightens the entertainment value of the theming, not the educational or historical aspects.

Holiday World has become a popular regional theme park with over one million visitors per year, and what is interesting about Holiday World, and telling of the dynamics of theming, is how the park references holidays. Unlike the specific references of Freedomland, Holiday World uses holiday referents in a fun, commonsensical and inexplicit manner. Some contemporary efforts to apply explicit theming like that of Freedomland – including a Hitler-themed restaurant in India and numerous Mao-themed ones in China – have met with controversy, in part due to their topics and in part to their being too specific in their referents.[30] Clearly, theming is a risky endeavour. Much like the moral attractions of Dreamland, the failure of Freedomland and the success of Holiday World may in part be attributed to the relative explicitness of the theming. When theming is too specific, a park may suffer from patrons who are

Patrons spin around and around aboard the HallowSwings at Holiday World.

unable or unwilling to grasp the referents involved, and when it is less explicit – when it evokes as opposed to invokes – it may be able to reach more people. In this last sense the theming of parks takes on the concept of mood.

In a comparison chart offered for the everyday vacationer Universal Studios Orlando expresses mood as it compares its attractions to those of its nearby competitor at Walt Disney World, Disney's Hollywood Studios and Disney's Animal Kingdom. Not only does Universal stress that it has more rides in many sections of its parks, but it stresses that its rides are *thrilling* – thus distinguishing itself from Disney parks, which offer nothing more than 'Yesterday's Classic Fairytales'.[31] In Universal's 'Vacation from the Ordinary' a theme park 'is more than a theme park'.[32] Universal Studios Orlando comprises two theme parks, Universal Studios Florida, which opened in 1990, and Islands of Adventure, which opened in 1999. Unlike many other theme parks these two utilize theming in a manner that does not pay attention to the explicit nature of place or geography. Instead specific moods that derive from experiences of visitors being able to 'Ride the Movies' orient a new form of theme park theming. In later years Universal Studios Florida made more explicit its attention to place, adding theme lands like Hollywood, World Expo, San Francisco/Amity and others, but the geographic referents are to locations in which certain movies were filmed or have loose associations with places. The park's Twister ride, for example, is located within the New York section while the World Expo features a Men in Black Alien Attack ride. What is significant is less the geography of the park than its referencing of major motion pictures, which arguably have become more cognitively etched in the minds of visitors than geographical locations. Continually, patrons are told that they can 'put themselves into the action of the movies', and in

this sense, interestingly, theming becomes a conceptual project, one that would be used with success in the quasi-theme parks of Las Vegas.

Whereas other theme parks ask customers to take a trip back in time, to revisit events of the past and to stroll in idyllic re-creations of places imagined and specific, Universal Studios Florida asks patrons to step inside conceptual spaces – ones that have already been reworked through the multiple permutations of motion pictures. In the case of the famous Jaws ride, visitors are not transported to the New England community of Martha's Vineyard, where *Jaws* was filmed, but to the fictional fishing vil-lage of Amity. Riders are thus twice removed in their thematic experience – first in the motion picture's representations of New England life, and second in the theme park's adaptation of the motion picture as a thrill ride. More and more, as cultural refer-ents mix, as media collide and as culture takes on the form of

At Universal Orlando patrons experience Poseidon's Fury, an interactive ride.

pastiche suggested by the philosopher Jean-François Lyotard, theme parks will utilize more meta or conceptual forms of theming that reference more the mood of a place, thing or quality, and further lessen the specific referents that have been used in the theming of the past.[33] As Michael Sorkin shows, the model of architecture and culture offered by Disney theme parks infects urbanism itself, creating cities based on Disney principles, while people, in their everyday negotiation of life, find themselves acting on and in space in a manner formerly reserved to the worlds of the theme park.[34] Additionally, parks like Universal utilize the passage of time and its increasing anachronistic effect to further distinguish themselves from Disney parks. This is a reversal of the strategy of Dreamland in which abundance and capital were used to challenge competitor parks; in this case, Universal strategically

Theme parks like Universal's Islands of Adventure juxtapose multiple architectural, technological and aesthetic modes in one space.

deploys concept, not capital, to challenge Disney: if Disney attractions are old-timey and stale, come to Universal where the attractions are current, exciting and hip.

As Walt Disney helped illustrate, it is possible to base a theme park on the life of an individual person and to use that celebrity's biography as a platform on which to theme an amusement park. Dollywood is one such park that in many respects outdoes Walt Disney's efforts to create a theme park based on biography. Originally opened as Silver Dollar City, the theme park was rethemed and reopened as Dollywood in 1986. The park is nestled in the scenic Smoky Mountains of Tennessee, and like the unthemed Knoebels in Elysburg, Pennsylvania, Dollywood utilizes the dialogue between the natural landscape (and all of its evocative associations) and the cultural aspects of the region as a means of theming the park.

A sign of authenticity – Dollywood's Grist Mill.

Unlike other theme parks Dollywood avoids the loop and instead arranges theme lands – including ones referencing river towns, jukeboxes, villages, canyons and the county fair – in a long strip, with one area that protrudes. Dollywood's press information reflects American archetypes – family, memory, God, the soul, the heart and the rustic. Like the Holy Land Experience in Orlando, Florida and Dickens World in Kent, UK, Dollywood focuses on successfully executing a thematic order that is manageable. It does not attempt to achieve a re-created map of the entire United States, as did Freedomland; instead it concentrates on key symbols or thematic archetypes on which to establish its amusement order. Like many theme parks Dollywood projects a clear theme through its many rides and attractions. River rapids rides reflect a reduction of the tension between the real Rocky Mountain outdoors and the theme park ride, while a water ride called Blazing Fury features a plot in which riders escape a fire in an 1880s town, suggesting a continuation of the theme park's emphasis on combining faux danger with relaxation and amusement. Another, the Mystery Mine, uses the image of Tennessee mining to create a themed roller coaster experience. Many of its rides effectively reference the park's overall themes, and even when they do not – as in the case of unthemed Ferris wheels, troikas and the like – Dollywood can connect these types of rides to the old-fashioned country tradition of the county fair. Thus even the unthemed is themed.

Dollywood celebrates Americana, country living and the persona of Dolly Parton throughout all of its attractions. Within its shops patrons can purchase items including baseball souvenirs, bald eagle items, pastoral Smoky Mountain artwork, old signs, handmade accent pieces, patriotic CDs and Christian books, and many of the shops reflect a thematic connection to Parton's biography, such as the Cas Walker store. The park intersperses a number of craft and heritage displays: 'Dollywood's master crafts-men and artisans proudly continue the centuries-old tradition of hand-making crafts in the Smoky Mountains with daily demon-strations.'[35] Lye soap making, slate roof tile production, wagon work and candle- and glass-making create a living portrait of authenticity that is used to establish a rhetorical connection to Dollywood's varied traditions. The park continues the tradition with numerous variety shows, including country, bluegrass, Christian and gospel music performances, and an overarching theme of reminiscence is suggested in the park's performances that ask patrons to 'take a nostalgic trip down memory lane'.[36] The park's numerous concessions offer customers a range of food choices, but only within the subset of Southern cooking – chicken, sausage, barbecue, pork rinds and flat bread sandwiches help establish the authentic order of the South, country living and mountain life. Like many theme parks Dollywood features annual events, including Christian and gospel music shows and a Smoky Mountain Christmas Festival.[37]

As a theme park Silver Dollar City was transformed with Dollywood's adoption of Dolly Parton's persona and its associated thematic elements. Like Walt Disney before her, Parton's star recognition provides a foundation for theming that is difficult to match in other non-person themed venues. A key to the theme park's ability to deliver its attractions is its biographical, person-centred theme.[38] Another is its attention to an effective theming complex, or the 'overall extent of theming development that is created throughout a venue, including architecture, decor, signage and the performances of costumed workers'.[39] Because of the park's complete integration of themed shows, performances, food, rides and historical memorabilia, Dollywood establishes an authentic order of theming that is not found in many amusement and theme parks. Its effective theming complex, like the quasi-theme parks of Las Vegas, allows it to create nuance, subtlety and believability throughout its themed space.

What the amusement park needed to compete with emerging forms of entertainment – including the otherworldliness of cinema and travel – was *a place*. By theming its venues with a variety of symbolic associations the theme park was on the move towards becoming its own place – just like the materiality of the city and the home, the theme park was no longer a substitute for other places, it was becoming its own. Walt Disney made the greatest impact on the theme park, in part because he applied formative principles – efficiency, cleanliness and capital investment – to the new theme park model that emerged in the late 1950s. Sharon Zukin notes that the success of Disney theme parks rests on their ability to transcend all other cultural identities and essentially forge a new 'national public culture'.[40] Other theme park companies followed, and what mattered was less the substance of how they achieved a sense of place – whether real or imagined, based on the life of a celebrity, focused on historical recreations or characteristic of a certain set of moods or feelings – but the fact that they aimed for *a* place. The amusement parks of Coney Island established a physical place for amusements, and they dabbled in historical recreations and amusement rides that referred to other locales – real and imaginary – but they failed to achieve the unifying vision that would later characterize the geography and architecture of Disneyland, Universal Studios, Dollywood and Six Flags Over Texas.

With Coney Island the amusement park 'emerges as a harbinger of modernity' and by the time the theme park takes hold in US society in the 1960s it makes the move towards becoming a functioning social form.[41] Its abundant and fantastic architecture is only one part of its approach, and when the partners of perform-ance, culture and symbolism are added, it is ready to enshrine itself in American society as a unique conveyor of reality, on a par with other indigenous American forms, including jazz. Unlike jazz the theme park lacks the social class and high art aesthetic con-notations that would codify it as a form of significance; instead it becomes the subject of ridicule, the bane of critics and taken for granted by the many who pass through its gates. Margaret King wrote that

> the theme park has displaced many older forms of amusement centers . . . and has sparked new trends in tourism, travel, recreation, family life and leisure economics. It has opened up new vistas and introduced new dimensions in other seemingly unrelated fields, such as television and film, highway and air travel, museums, world's fairs, urban planning, theater, set design, environmental planning, ecological experimentation, civil engineering and architecture, both private and public.[42]

As an architectural and social form, the theme park is more than a means of entertainment, in fact by the late twentieth century it is a fully functional form that competes with cinema, theatre, tele-vision and literature for hold of the popular consumer imagination. Wrongly seen by many as merely an entertainment form, it is indeed a life form – a means of negotiating the self, the world around it and the vast expanse of culture, people and things in the world.

3 Theme Park as Machine

People are exactly alike when they ride amusements – they react the same way, get the same thrills and pleasures.
Roller coaster designer Harry G. Traver[1]

There is something remarkable about images of the roller coaster. Viewing a still photograph of a roller coaster provides an interesting moment in time of the theme park: the motion of riders is frozen, the tracks are still and the trains of the roller coaster are stationary. On the surface, close inspection of the roller coaster reveals the ridiculous. People are strapped into a mechanical device that carries them up hills, drops them, and then wraps them around numerous twists and turns. What other species would be capable of building a machine that produces amusement effects directly on the body and the mind? In everyday life, outside the world of the theme park, people use the term 'roller coaster' to refer to situations of upheaval, moments of an up-and-down nature, and turbulence and disorder. The roller coaster, unlike most other forms of public amusements, becomes a figure of life – not simply a device used to propel people along the tracks of an amusement park, but an expression of life itself. Sometimes, life is like a roller coaster, the ride embodied beyond its material consequences perhaps suggests. And as a metaphor the still photograph of the roller coaster offers something even more profound: it illustrates how life runs in moments and, just as one part of life is enjoyed, it is gone and the next one is around the hill. Like many aspects of the theme park the roller coaster is at once mundane and sublime, functional and symbolic.

It is impossible to consider the transformation of the theme park from the pleasure gardens, the world's fairs and the early amusement parks of Coney Island without considering the significance of the machine. The machine is both the amusement park's and the theme park's *raison d'être* – it gives both a life force, yet is used differently in each. In the amusement park it is a thing of sensory and kinetic delight, it throws people together and reminds them of their mortality, while in the theme park it is often a part of the story being told through theming, something that affects the body but also the mind. Interestingly, the greatest tension in the evolution of the amusement park into the theme park occurs with the ride. In the twenty-first century – which is resolutely a time of the theme park – some throwbacks or amusement atavists exist. These are the parks that dare offer themselves up not as theme parks, but as amusement parks, and they do this primarily through the promotion not of the theme but of the

A journey aboard the roller coaster at Coney Island, here frozen in time.

machine. Indeed, the amusement machine is the last stand of the amusement park in the world of theme parks.

Even before the early Russian ice slide that would become the roller coaster, the carousel emerged in the twelfth century in Arab countries as a game of horsemen involving a clay ball filled with scented water, eventually being called 'carrosello', literally 'little war', in Spain and Italy and later 'carrousel' in France.[2] When it became adopted in French society, lavish carousels were viewed by the public, involving incredible spectacles of safe horsemanship that replaced the bloody jousts of the past. One of the features of the carousel was known as 'catching the brass ring', and it included horsemen who would demonstrate their competency by spearing brass rings on their lances. To practise for their tournaments, which featured real horses, devices were installed in royal courts. On such devices, two men operated a circular machine by hand while two riders, mounted on wooden horses, practised

On the Scenic Railway, the terrifying kinetics of the new amusement machines.

spearing the brass rings. Eventually this practice device became one of public amusement. The human-operated carousel was replaced with a horse- or mule-powered system that carried children around in circles to the delight of their parents and those watching. These early machines had no platforms, and thus the name 'flying horses' described a machine in which riders were suspended in the air. By the 1800s steam power was introduced, the carousel was given a platform, carousel animals moved up and down in tandem with the centripetal motion (giving them a gallop like real horses) and organ music was added as a further sensory stimulation.

The carousel thus gives the theme park its very first machine. It is a pleasure device of extraordinary principles. Not only does it move, creating a sensory swirl for children and parents alike, it is an

The carousel combines the powerful symbolism of animals with the kinetic thrill of moving in circles.

aesthetic device. Countless hours went into the production of the sculpted and painted horses of designers like those of Dentzel, Looff, Landow and Herschell, and even for the public they became an immediate obsession: it is reported that one man was so taken with the carousel that he mortgaged all of his possessions, including his farm and cows, just to invest in one.[3] The carousel is an architectural machine: its circularity is highlighted by the animals, their vertical movements up and down, the bright colours of animals and superstructure alike, and the calliope music, which is its own machine within a machine, providing another anachronistic look at the amusement parks of old. The carousel is a heritage device and, like the roller coaster, is the immediate concern of preservationists who long for an amusement park full of old-time machines. At extant amusement parks like Knoebels in Pennsylvania, elaborate museums have been established to showcase the wonder of carousels of the past, and the park's current carousels feature actual 'catching the brass ring' devices that allow riders to experience the symbolism of the original horse tournaments.

Most importantly for the amusement park, the carousel is immediately recognizable; it is as iconic to amusement patrons as the stone tool may have been to early humans. As one writer suggests, 'Everybody knows the carousel or merry-go-round . . . its riders are in a dream; for a whole minute they imagine themselves in a higher sphere.'[4] Its notoriety as a device that could send people into obsessive quests to own one or at least gaze at its movements, sounds and delights, established it as an important centrepiece for the amusement park. At the New York World's Fair of 1964–5, a 'Carousel Park' was created to feature the device as the prominent centre around which people could enjoy food and merriment. In later amusement parks the machine via its visual, kinetic and auditory effects signalled to people that safe, fun and family-centred amusement was

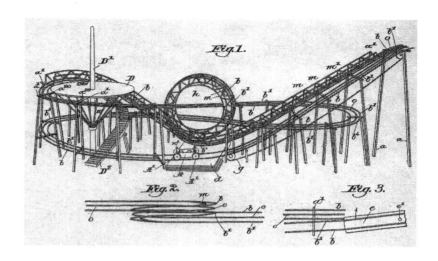

present in the park which featured it. Later the carousel would decline in popularity, and in the twenty-first century theme park its appearance is rare. In the complex theming that took hold in the theme park the carousel was ultimately unable to be incorporated. What becomes clear is that like the amazing carousel ride, the theme park is, itself, a larger machine; one composed of all the various rides, mechanical devices, subsystems, processes and performances that make up its functional system.[5] Just as the carousel ride could break down and bring stark attention to the mechanical artificiality that it created, so too could the theme park.

Like the roller coaster schematic, the theme park map exposes an interesting mechanical truth of the theme park. As the previous chapter discussed, the emergence of the theme park involved its finding of a place-based identity, and part and parcel of this identity was the map that it offered for the patron. At pleasure gardens and world's fairs zones separating various parts of the space were

The roller coaster, with its unparalleled ability to throw riders in multiple positions in space, gives the theme park its most important machine. E. Prescott, Roller Coaster, US patent, 1898.

Being thrown aboard a ride is just one of the ways that theme parks promote dissociation from the real world.

created, and at later amusement parks of Coney Island, people were given a sense of space as certain rides and attractions promised trips to other places or time periods. With the emergence of theme parks in the late 1950s maps were carefully constructed by theme park designers and, most significantly, these were cognitive maps that attempted to locate the park's attractions and its overall layout in the minds of the customers. Predictability of the patron, such as what she would do after she exited a ride, was codified in the park's geography. Later, as the theme park became a multi-use themed space in the 1990s, cognitive maps were drawn to include the minute sensory coordinates of patrons on the map.

In many contemporary theme parks the feeling of geographic disassociation is used to create thrill in the patron and generate profits in the company. In most cases this feeling is illusionary since the patron soon discovers that she has been walking in a loop. Getting lost in a theme park – or later, getting lost in a themed casino – becomes the subject of folk discussions among patrons. Just as one relates harrowing experiences of foreign travel with others, the theme park patron expresses how getting lost – in both the sense of geographical misdirection and visual and sensory bombardment from the park's attractions – was part of the fun of being in the theme park. In modern theme parks like Six Flags employees are trained that one of the most important interactions with patrons is giving them the correct directions to an attraction. Giving them the wrong information results in them getting lost, becoming unhappy and losing time in their day of park enjoyment. As the patron walks through a theme park, and 'moves from ride to ride, he or she is always caught in a web of references to other rides, and ultimately, to the theme park as a whole'.[6] Architecture was used to create ambience in early parks and in later themed ones it creates thematic mood. Patrons, as they move from one

place to another, are also caught up in a system of references that connects them to the design order of the theme park. As much as a person comes to the theme park with his own identity, due to passing through the map of the park and all of its nodes, he must supplant his identity with the themes, rides and functions of the park. A tension thus develops, and it is one that is endemic to cybernetics (relations of humans and machines) whether in a theme park or not. This is one in which the person must respond to the delights provided by machines – rides, robots and other devices – and to the overall 'machine', that is, the theme park, all the while being able to enjoy himself in a non-mechanical sense.

The cybernetics of the early amusement park – in which people were often assaulted by machines like those of Tilyou's Steeplechase – gave way to a version that lessened the harsh kinetic impacts of rides on bodies and increased the use of rides as story, as a means of placing patrons inside a narrative machine. Because new theme

Being lost, being found – all conditioned by the geographic machine of the theme park.

parks comprise 'lands' and are not simply assemblages of rides and amusements, people take on a new relationship to architecture and landscape. Just like an explorer who encounters new varieties of flora and fauna and experiences disassociation, the theme park patron is trying to navigate through artificial mazes, simulated facades and unaccustomed experiences. As a result techniques of cybernetic adjustment develop. Theme park guidebooks are themselves a fledgling industry, and many of them detail the best touring plan for the patron. Advice on how to get to the park, whether by air or car, tips for navigating through the park (including shortcuts), strategies for beating or avoiding the crowds, ideas about which line to take in a ride queue house (such as, 'Always take the left line when given a choice'), and when to visit certain rides and attractions during the touring day are all the lengthy subjects of such guidebooks. Such plans have led some theme park patrons to joke, 'This seems more like work than fun', and such comments further highlight the tension of the human and the mechanical. Beginning in 1999 Disney theme parks incorporated a system known as 'FAST-PASS'. In this system a patron receives a ticket that tells him when he may come back and ride a particular ride and thus programmes all of his activities for the day, based on when he can visit the specific rides. Some individuals, hoping to optimize their travels through theme parks, have employed forms of artificial intelligence. In one case a man used such computer-based technology to visit each of the 41 rides, attractions and shows at Disney's Magic Kingdom in just over ten hours.[7] Such examples of cybernetic adjustment will no doubt continue as the theme park evolves. Undoubtedly they will further raise awareness about the difficult tension between the desire of patrons to enjoy theme parks in free, non-mechanical ways and the desire of the theme park to manage, control and determine patron behaviour in mechanistic ways.

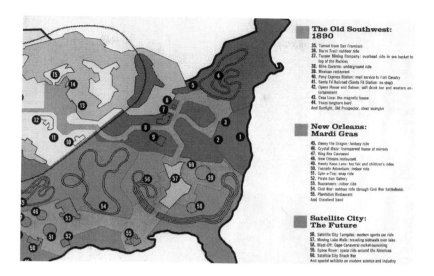

The Old Southwest: 1890

35. Tunnel from San Francisco
36. Burro Trail: outdoor ride
37. Tucson Mining Company: overhead ride in ore bucket to top of the Rockies
38. Mine Caverns: underground ride
39. Mexican restaurant
40. Pony Express Station: mail service to Fort Cavalry
41. Santa Fé Railroad (Santa Fé Station: no stop)
42. Opera House and Saloon: soft drink bar and western entertainment
43. Casa Loca: the magnetic house
44. Texas longhorn herd
And Gunfight, Old Prospector, steer wrangler

New Orleans: Mardi Gras

45. Danny the Dragon: fantasy ride
46. Crystal Maze: transparent house of mirrors
47. King Rex Carousel
48. New Orleans restaurant
49. Kandy Kane Lane: toy fair and children's rides
50. Tornado Adventure: indoor ride
51. Spin-a-Top: snap ride
52. Pirate Gun Gallery
53. Buccaneers: indoor ride
54. Civil War: outdoor ride through Civil War battlefields
55. Plantation Restaurant
And Dixieland band

Satellite City: The Future

56. Satellite City Turnpike: modern sports car ride
57. Moving Lake Walk: traveling sidewalk over lake
58. Blast-Off: Cape Canaveral rocket-launching
59. Space Rover: space ride around the Americas
60. Satellite City Snack Bar
And special exhibits on modern science and industry

The roller coaster, like the carousel, is a foundational component of the theme park. It is architectural, in that it features a superstructure and numerous design features and is situated within a geographical landscape, but it is also mechanical in that it moves people along a track. Devices called ice slides used in Russia in the 1600s are often considered to be the ancestors of the roller coaster, but though they bore resemblances to the amusement park roller coaster, they were not machines in the fullest sense of the term. These early slides were limited in their kinetic effects on riders. Later examples of the fledgling machine included slides that propelled people down wooden hills, allowing people to enjoy the same ride in the summer.[8] In 1804 the first prototype coaster was constructed near Paris, with important advancements like tracks and carriages complete with wheels. Later designs would make the roller coaster more practical, as it was inconvenient to ask riders to climb to the top of platforms just to descend

A map of the defunct theme park Freedomland: nodes, zones, points of connection.

down a hill. The Centrifugal Pleasure Railway, a device premiered at France's Frascati Gardens in 1848, featured a loop that propelled riders upside down.[9] This must have been an amazing visual and kinetic thrill at the time, especially given the initial concern about the French workman who tested the ride for its first run. It was reported that onlookers took up a collection for his family in case he died while trying the looping coaster.[10] It is important to note that such a sense of adventure was only possible in a time of mechanical invention. In today's world safe leisure experiences have led to some seeking out more dangerous and dark forms of tourism, such as travelling to dangerous places or partaking in extreme sports like base jumping, white water rapids rides and so on.

The roller coaster came to the United States in 1843 in the form of the Mauch Chunk Railway, a coal mine car that was converted into a thrilling runaway train ride. In 1885 LaMarcus Thompson was the first to patent a roller coaster. In the years that followed roller coasters developed swiftly. As new amusement parks sprang up, they often included one or more prominent roller coasters – which in turn helped establish the unique character of the park – and continued

The primogeniture of the modern roller coaster – the Mauch Chunk switchback railway.

technological developments, like upstop wheels and tubular steel, allowed more fantastic roller coasters to be built. Some of the earliest, including the first loop-the-loop at Coney Island, the Flip Flap, were considerably more menacing machines than those of the present. Some reports indicate that due to the perfect loops created on such rides, riders would experience as many as 12 Gs (the force resulting from acceleration) during the loop.[11] Like the fierce early loop-the-loops Harry G. Traver's Crystal Beach Cyclone, opened in 1927, often produced notable effects in riders, including dizziness, fainting and head, chest and leg injuries.[12] The roller coaster featured a nurse on duty to deal with any complications from the ride. In one unfortunate case, a man was thrown from it and dragged to his death; one person commented at the time that 'I saw a body hurtle through the air but at first thought it was just an overcoat. Then I heard piercing screams.'[13] Later design technology allowed for the creation of tamer roller coasters, much to the disappointment of some riders who long for the days of monstrous machines like the Traver Cyclone.[14] Traver, who longed to publish an anthropological/philosophical text, *Earth, Life, and*

The incredible Crystal Beach Cyclone of Harry G. Traver, which some call the only avant-garde roller coaster ever built.

Man, but never did, probably used his mechanical expertise as a way to explore basic human needs, desires and tendencies.[15] The roller coaster proved to be the perfect testing grounds for analysing the essentials of the human condition – fear, desire, safety, ecstasy and so on.

Like other theme park technologies, including the robot, the roller coaster creates fascination in the form of black box aesthetics; as Jean Baudrillard said of machines, 'functioning is not merely the function of things but also their mystery'.[16] Videos, television shows, scientific websites and books detail ways that teachers can utilize the roller coaster in a pedagogical sense. Physics teachers, for example, can use roller coasters to teach many of the principles of gravity, acceleration and G-force. The roller coaster established a fascination with engineering and the machine that would ironically influence the adoption of non-theme park machine technologies in society. Learning about a machine like a roller coaster, and understanding all of its technical terms – upstop wheels, lift hill, station brakes, chain dog – becomes a primary concern of roller coaster aficionados. For many such fans the excitement of learning about famous roller coasters on the Internet and in amusement park history books and the fashioning of their own homemade, working models of roller coasters, is heightened by the actual riding of the rides in the park. Such excitement takes on the order of religious pilgrimage as fans opt to spend large sums of money travelling the world to ride as many famous roller coasters as possible. As one member of the American Coaster Enthusiasts offered, 'I'll never stop riding roller coasters. I started when I was eight years old and I'll ride until the day I die. I'll travel wherever it takes to ride a new one. When I run out in the United States, I'll go to another country to ride.'[17]

While the carousel established itself as an aesthetic and heritage device, it did so in a generic way. People do not necessarily attach personality to the carousel but with the roller coaster a new dimension of the theme park machine develops. In this case each machine has a different personality. People assess differences between wooden and steel tube versions, they decide what time of the day to ride the coaster (to maximize speed and visceral effects on the body) and they consider whether riding in the front or the back car is best. Their assessments get even more specific, beyond these design elements, as they begin to make mental lists of the best roller coasters and as they associate personal qualities with rides. In an intimate relationship – 'that one kicked my ass, but I love it' – soon the roller coaster is anthropomorphized, in part assisted by new forms of theming that name and further personalize roller coasters. Roller coasters, as semiotic objects, reflect a world that is beyond amusement itself. The passivity of life – whether working

Aboard the Griffon at Busch Gardens Europe: fright, weightlessness, the push of the Earth back on the body and joy all combine in one moment on the roller coaster.

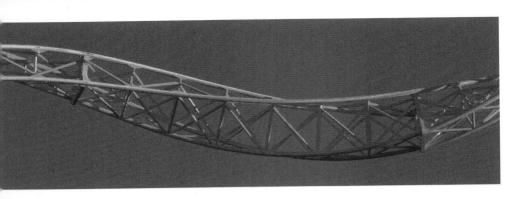

in an office building or sitting in front of a television – is contrasted with imagery of violent nature, uncharted and adventurous spaces and journeys, and technological and animalistic vitality. Names of roller coasters reflect this – the mythical creatures and figures of the Griffon, Loch Ness Monster, Hydra, Banshee, Medusa, Sea Serpent, Dragon, Poltergeist, Kraken, Titan, Kong, Demon, Zeus; fierce animals like the Viper, Great Bear, Python, Scorpion, Grizzly, Rattler, King Cobra; forces of nature like Tidal Wave, Windstorm, Wild Lightnin', Wicked Twister, Vortex, Volcano, Turbulence; forms of technology, conditions and objects that connote power, speed and ability, like Excalibur, Top Gun, XLR-8, Shockwave, Fahrenheit, Jet Coaster, Speed, Roar. Roller coasters do far more than remind us who we are; they tell us who we wish to be and thus they speak of our existential and psychological needs as much as our basic values.

The roller coaster is the first amusement ride to be integrated into people's lives in an intimate way. Nostalgia for them invites couples to discuss their first ride on a coaster and how it later led to marriage, while others decide to take their vows on a roller coaster. As CNN reported, 'Some couples face the inevitable ups and downs of matrimony head-on – they get married on roller coasters'.[18] In other cases roller coaster enthusiasts attempt to set endurance records by riding for hours on the machines without a break. In an interesting

The roller coaster, captured like a double helix in space, gives a sense of its foundational and genetic role in the theme park.

meeting of human relationships and machines, the roller coaster seems to pronounce a metaphorical understanding – just like the ups and downs of marriage and social relationships, the roller coaster is an experience that must be endured but, after a while, the rider will come to enjoy all of the bumps.

Roller coasters also indicate an inability to persist. They tell a different story, not of overcoming obstacles but of being overcome by the machine. In a very conceptual moment, John Allen, former president of the famed Philadelphia Toboggan Company, once said that 'the ultimate roller coaster is built when you send out twenty-four people and they all come back dead. This could be done, you know'.[19] Allen's comment, meant in jest, is nonetheless an interesting reflection on the machine and the human. Feature films like *Rollercoaster* (1977) and *Thrill* (1996) use the roller coaster as a device for establishing horror, terror and suspense in the film viewer, and directors choose this amusement machine as the catalyst of such moods because of its prominent role in the amusement and theme park. They suggest that as easily as such devices can give people pleasure, they can take it away. Though roller coaster accidents and deaths do occur they are very rare, but this does not stop the public from reflecting on, if not obsessing over, the idea of a catastrophic roller coaster failure or accident. Once, working on the XLR-8 roller coaster at Six Flags AstroWorld, I was charged with calming customers during a situation in which the coaster became stalled at the top of the ride's lift hill. At such moments riders realize that the cost of their desire to be thrilled is high and, ultimately, that they have little autonomy when strapped into a mechanical device of their own will.

Because the roller coaster and the amusement park are so intimately connected, and because the presence of the thrill ride may suggest less reliance on theming and mood landscapes within a

park, it is not surprising that Disney theme parks immediately opposed themselves to the device. After Disneyland and subsequent theme parks were opened, patrons complained that Disney parks were lacking, notably because they had no real roller coasters. Though their parks featured some prominent ones, such as Space Mountain, Matterhorn Bobsleds and Big Thunder Mountain Railroad, people felt that these were thematic delivery devices rather than true white knuckle rides. Only at Disney's California Adventure Park did the company finally cave in and build a primary roller coaster, California Screamin'. What the roller coaster indicates is the uneasy tension that is still present between the amusement park and the theme park. For some patrons, like many of the American Coaster Enthusiasts (ACE) and the Roller Coaster

At Coney Island a ride down the Razzle Dazzle expresses the pleasure of the body in space.

Club of Great Britain (RCCGB), what signifies a theme park should not be the theming of its attractions, but its ability to deliver heart-pounding and innovative rides, especially roller coasters. As long as the roller coaster exists, it will continue to mediate the greatest of tensions between the atavistic amusement park and the contemporary themed park.[20] As one roller coaster designer said, the roller coaster has the most personality and potential of all theme park machines: 'You don't know what's gonna happen, you're just letting the coaster take control of you.'[21]

The experience of being on a ride suspends the conventions of everyday life. For the individual, the ride offers an out-of-body experience of an ecstatic nature, while for the social body, as George Tilyou pioneered, the ride's ability to throw people together negated the normal social order and asked people to see, and be with, others in a new way. Rides thus became an 'othering' experience in which people came into contact with people in forms of intimacy previously reserved for family and friends. In a personal sense being on a ride enacts a similar suspension of normality. Riding a roller coaster or a troika involves a liminal state – being betwixt and between, being in the womb, being in the midst of things, expressing the most extreme human emotions, fear, death, danger, sex, ecstasy. In this way a theme park ride discards both the social and psychological orders of the day; it is as revolutionary, if not more so, than the greatest works of art.

Like theme park planners, ride designers focus on creating rides and technological attractions that combine kinetic and experiential thrills, safety, efficiency and throughput. Like other mechanical artists they are limited only by technology and capital in their attempts to produce the next great ride, the one that will define their theme park. In the case of the roller coaster, with each major technological advance – upstop wheels, tubular steel, pipeline, suspended rides, urethane wheels, linear induction motor, inverted rides – new ride families are born, and with each techno-logical development comes new mythologies – the first coaster over 300 feet (90 metres), the first one to exceed 100 miles (160 km). One theme park journalist commented on this trend, saying, 'We're in the roller coaster arms race . . . Every park likes to have bragging rights to the fastest, wildest ride for at least one year.'[22] Parks like Cedar Point in Sandusky, Ohio continually design and build new coasters (seventeen in 2008, then the world's most in a park), and in the case of this park, which most consider an amuse-ment park, explicit theming is avoided. Instead roller coasters provide a thematic and mechanic orientation for a park that dubs itself 'America's Roller Coast'. While part of the mechanical arms race may be attributed to the desires of consumers to attain some-thing new in a consumerist world, another part may be attributed to the powerful myths that are created as new rides are designed, built and opened. With each ride design anticipation for the next ride mounts. On Internet fan and blog sites ride enthusiasts discuss rumours surrounding planned attractions or, in some cases, debate the merits of ride alterations, such as retheming a ride, demolish-ing it or selling it to another park. In some cases enthusiasts mount national or even international campaigns to save rides from demolition and some gain status as National Historic Landmarks in the United States.

Theme park rides, in no small part due to the prominent role of ride designers and builders, achieve a mythopoetic status. For enthusiasts riding a famous roller coaster is like travelling to a site of religious significance. Even for the non-enthusiast – the every-day rider or theme park visitor – the roller coaster or park ride can have a magical status, in part due to its black box aesthetics and the sense of mystery and danger attached to rides. Theme park

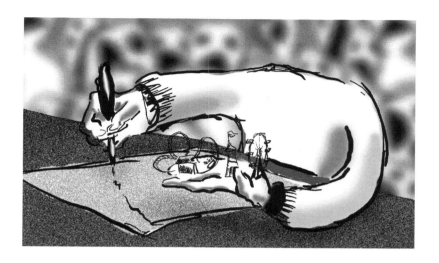

documentaries can damage this aesthetic by exposing the inside of a ride, showing us how it works, and thus lessening the suspense that comes when we board a ride. This lessening of the aesthetic can also have consequences in terms of safety perceptions. When a theme park trainer at AstroWorld and someone who frequently operated the rides on busy days, I was accustomed to the issue of safety. Stories of gruesome deaths and terrible accidents were the subject of water cooler talk among veteran and new employees. Ride safety was such a concern that employees who made major safety blunders were almost immediately fired. Employees were taught to watch all areas of the ride – if the ride was moving and someone jumped off or if someone entered the ride area while the ride was in motion, the attendant had to immediately stop the ride and call security. There are few arenas in any society in which teenagers are charged with the operation of multi-million dollar machines of incredible power and potential danger. For visitors to the theme park the danger of the ride (its black box aesthetics) is

The work of theme park designers is always a mental quest to materialize the dreams of the mind in the material creations of rides, park technologies and attractions.

part of the thrill involved in riding it, but that danger must end with simulation. While theme park workers are trained in the minute details of ride operation – such as a 'push down, pull up' of the lapbars on the ride – for the visitor the perception that rides are unsafe or that workers are unskilled is often paramount. In the United States, in part due to poor safety conditions at non-theme park venues (for example, bungee jumping) and to the telescoping effect that occurs when a ride malfunctions, legislation has been developed to deal with ride safety.[23] While no one wants to be injured or killed on a ride, the mandating of strict safety procedures may further lessen the black box aesthetics of the theme park ride and decrease the theme park's Dionysian tendencies.

For workers in the theme park, there are two primary emphases – one is making certain that the patron is happy, the other is to attend to the safety of the patron. Most theme park accidents are the result of patron negligence, not worker or mechanical failure, yet, in popular culture, television shows often reflect an obsession with the theme park accident. Though in many nations automobiles result in astronomically more deaths and injuries, theme park accidents receive much more attention. In the United States when a roller coaster becomes stuck for a substantial period of time it is often broadcast live on national news. Lewis Mumford wrote of the machine that as much as it reflects humankind's immortality, 'it is often an indication of ineptitude and social paralysis'.[24] It is likely that the theme park accident reflects an existential anxiety about machines as well as a general psychological association of pleasure and death.[25] The early amusement parks of Coney Island also illustrated this fascination with death and pleasure, but in the reenactments of Fighting the Flames and the Galveston Flood, which were more representational and conceptual. In today's theme park, where safety and security have emerged as primary concerns in 'risk society', death, injury and the breakdown are real-world categories projected onto the amusement activities of theme park patrons.[26]

It is no surprise that in theme park video games of the sort considered in chapter Six success almost always amounts to being able to run one's fictional theme park as a machine. An assumption shared by both theme park managers and theme park patrons is that the theme park operates like a machine. The theme park, in

their minds, becomes a representation of Herbert Spencer's social organism, a system that self-regulates and whose ultimate goal is to keep itself running. However, beneath the surface of any theme park, as Thad Donovan's surrealistic artwork suggests, there is a sinister absence. In the minds of people who frequent theme parks there are often fears of malfunctioning rides and surly or dangerous park workers.[27] In popular culture theme parks are often related to the breakdown – a situation in which things go terribly wrong. It often takes a breakdown of a theme park ride for the individual to realize the artifice that is in play. Like the still shot

Regardless of the efforts of designers, managers, workers and even patrons, the theme park projects its own desires beneath its surfaces.

of the roller coaster the breakdown provides for a moment of reflection on the machine and the park. In popular film and television the park breakdown is seen as something horrifying and sometimes comedic. In a parody of the theme park in the popular show *The Simpsons* the Itchy & Scratchy World Park is run by robots that run amok and turn the park into a land of fears. As much as theme parks reflect a sense of control and precision, they also project the opposite: chaos and apprehension.

At historic Coney Island visitors became accustomed to the architectural spectacle of the Iron Tower. After descending it, patrons could drink milk from the mechanical udders of a fake cow. Such examples of mechanical animals and gag devices suggested that the evolution of the theme park would involve more than the use of the machine to provide corporeal and kinaesthetic amusements; like the facade of architecture that made up the amusement buildings of Coney Island, machines themselves could be used to fulfill aesthetic, symbolic and social purposes. At the world's fairs, including the Century of Progress (1933) and the World Tomorrow (1939), companies like Messmore & Damon produced mechanical amusements that would later find their way to the theme park. Audiences at the world's fairs were stunned by life-sized mechanical elephants, ferocious moving dinosaurs and lifelike dioramas that suggested a fusion of ambient landscapes and recreated machines. With new technological advances in both mechanical science and scenic and interior design fantasy spaces could be produced with greater ease. Now it was possible to do more than re-create a landscape from the past or from a distant location; it was possible to create robotic animals, people and fantasy creatures.

Just as the roller coaster provided a kinetic form of architecture for the amusement park, the amusement machine gave it a sense

of performance. As people exited the moving architecture of roller coasters, their eyes were met with more movement in the form of mechanized amusements. Like the exotic real people from the world's fairs' midways, these exotic machines gave people something to gawk at. On the surface they acted as visual forms of the sublime – 'look at that mechanical elephant . . . it's lifelike' – and beneath they forged a new black box aesthetic, that of 'how'd they do that'? Whereas the ethnological exoticism of the parades of people at the fairs produced amazement without desire to know, the new mechanical aesthetics of the amusement park combined surface amazement with a desire to understand how the machine produced its illusions. And, where the roller coaster symbolized the inhuman side of the amusement park – the out of control machine – the mechanized device offered its ironically human side, the robot that looks human but is not.

The most pronounced applications of robotics are coterminous with the founding of the first major theme park, Disneyland. At the 1964–5 New York World's Fair, Walt Disney proved that a robotic

The robot, like this one designed for themed attractions, provides an uncanny connection to human forms and spaces.

human could mesmerize people. What was needed was a way to incorporate the robot into the theme lands of the theme park. In an early Disney-era film on the concept it is suggested that Disney's interest in the robot was moving from the two-dimensional animation of the cartoon into the three-dimensional realm of the moving machine. Audio-animatronics reflect Disney's desire to create life-like, believable characters that would fulfil both mechanical desires – for efficient workers that did not have to be paid – and organic desires – for a friendly three-dimensional cartoon character who had personality and who could tell a story or otherwise fit into a narrative or thematic approach. Much like the motion capture technology that would later dominate the video game industry, Disney worked with engineers to attempt to duplicate the movements of actors and dancers like Buddy Ebsen in mechanical models. In numerous attractions, like Pirates of the Caribbean, the Hall of Presidents and Country Bear Jamboree, Disney helped illustrate that 'robots are clever, precise, and fun . . . Above all, they are entertaining and not to be feared'.[28] Not all theme parks enjoy Disney's capital, and thus they have to produce less elaborate robotics and other mechanical amusement devices to entertain the patron. What the robot establishes for all theme parks is an emphasis on a mechanical form that is at once entertaining and strangely real.

The history of the dark ride dates to 1901 where at the Pan-American Exposition A Trip to the Moon gave people the thrill of travel without travelling. The terror of the indoor ride is built not on the disorientation of being spun around or being thrown back and forth, like troikas and ship rides, nor does it rely on the violence of speed alone, as with the roller coaster. Instead it uses darkness and isolation and all that they symbolically entail to create its thrills. In some cases the dark ride is not dark at all, as in Disney's It's a Small World, but the effects of disorientation and

Luna Park's popular Helter Skelter ride, where people were thrown in ways previously unknown to them.

seeming to travel to some other place are heightened by the enclosure provided by the dark ride. As the theme park moves further away from the kinetic thrills of the traditional amusement ride like the roller coaster, it builds on the dark ride's potential to use its enclosure and interior design to create a narrative and thematic space. While inside the dark ride, one is literally taken into another world. Like the modern themed casino's use of themed architecture as a space of isolation, the dark ride achieves the otherworldly by locking people inside another world and by detailing this world through special effects and interior design.

The dark ride includes many variants: rides that operate on tracks (such as old mill rides), rides that float through water (such as the famous Disney Pirates of the Caribbean), fun houses that feature gags and bodily amusements, walk-through rides (like the famous Noah's Ark), while the most contemporary and expensive

The dark ride Revenge of the Mummy at Universal Orlando uses the human fear of the dark and the unexpected to achieve extraordinary emotional thrills.

are simulation rides that take thematic experience to a new high-tech dimension. In whichever form the dark ride may be considered the most liminal of rides in the park; it is also the most psychological. The experience of going through the ride is heightened by the separation that occurs shortly after boarding: one is removed by the darkness from the space of the living, symbolized by light. The darkness takes hold of the rider, and around each turn of the car is an unexpected occurrence. Such a ride attempts to build on both expectation and surprise, capturing the rider in a simulated space of terror: 'It's kind of like a survival journey. Images of death, despair, destruction, of fright are being thrown at you, but you survive it. It's a very positive experience in the end because you have escaped that terror.'[29]

What makes the dark ride so significant for the theme park is its ability to deliver sensory experiences. One of the most profound influences of the theme park on contemporary consumer space involves the senses, specifically the ability to connect with consumers in the most intimate of possible ways. A Trip to the Moon was revolutionary in that it allowed people to freely experience a space; in a sense, they were given more control of the experience of the amusement story, or at least the illusion of control. As amusement technology develops parks deploy sensory technologies to further give patrons the sense of being inside a story. Blasts of air hit the body, people feel sprays of water, they are treated to unique smells, the heat sensation of fire hits their bodies, they ride in devices in which their balance is thrown off, and sounds of all varieties come from all angles. At the now closed ExtraTERRORestrial Alien Encounter of Disney, illusions of aliens licking patrons were made possible by high technology. Perhaps most significant for the dark ride and its use of sensory techniques is the emphasis on cinematic modes.

Like pacing in film, the newest dark rides use the unexpected – a quick turn of the ride and a sudden jolt of a monster, scene or other sight – to heighten the sensory experience of the ride. Similar to jump cuts in film, ride pacing creates constant visual and kinetic situations, sometimes so fast that the rider is unaware of what is happening. The most current use of cinema in the dark ride is exemplified by rides like Disney's Tower of Terror, which uses the successful *Twilight Zone* TV series to connect patrons to larger and predetermined narratives, and embellishes the experiences with the use of holographic ghosts and surprises like a ride vehicle that moves from a horizontal plane to a vertical one and back again. Modern rides also use audio-animatronic technologies, as in Pirates of the Caribbean and the Haunted Mansion at Disney theme parks. In such cases characters played by the robots extend the interest in story or cinematic narrative. While some traditional fun houses create sensory experiences only though quick shocks and generic references to ghosts, dungeons and demons, in the newest dark rides technology provides the possibility of creating entire narratives, which though only lasting a few minutes nevertheless give patrons the sense of having entered and then exited another world. At Universal Orlando's E. T. Adventure, for example, people experience the entirety of a story from start to finish, including E. T.'s adventures on Earth and his return to his home planet. Motion based simulation, in which filmic images on a screen connect to the motion of a ride simulator (as in Back to the Future: The Ride at Universal Studios), further heightens the sense of story, sensory immersion and the connection between the riders and the scenarios being staged.

In his assessment of the state of amusement parks in 1904 Edwin Slosson wrote of the peculiar similarity of amusement park rides and the machines of everyday life: 'that curious disposition

of people to make their amusements so like their daily life . . . The switchbacks, scenic railways and toy trains are merely trolley cars.'[30] Though the amusement parks of Slosson's era purported to create another world, at the same time they reflected the real world in which they were embedded. The mechanistic aesthetic of Coney Island's parks both celebrated and cautiously analysed the increasing cybernetics of humans and machines. It also reflected the desire of people to experiment with new interpersonal forms, a social machine of sorts.

As people were physically thrown together on human roulette wheels, human pool tables and other sorts of kinetic thrills, they were socially thrown in close proximity with one another. Edward Tilyou, son of Steeplechase's George Tilyou, once remarked that Coney Island acted as a 'gigantic laboratory of human nature'.[31]

Rides like the Amazing Adventures of Spider-Man at Universal Orlando create an experience that combines the approaches of theme parks and films in one space.

The mechanical rides of Coney gave people the opportunity to experiment, and as these were so popular and as they became so intertwined in people's lives, relationships and emotions, they actually helped forge a new social age. One of the most important

The popular Dew Drop at Steeplechase Park threw people down a slide, causing them to reflect on their own bodies and the bodies of others.

functions these rides served was to bring men and women together. Many couples met at Coney Island amusement parks or chose them as a place to spend their first time together. Later, upon marrying, they would reflect on the joy that the parks provided them and how they allowed them to meet, frolic and better understand one another. Edwin E. Slosson ends his survey of 1904 Coney Island, 'The Amusement Business', with an emphasis on the role that Coney played as a matchmaker: 'Many a young couple have been so well satisfied with each other in this short journey through Coney Island that they have decided to continue traveling together though life.'[32] The contemporary theme park also serves a social role, but it differs in its approach. Disney theme parks, in particular, shifted the

A view of Blackpool's famous amusement zone, a place of popular amusement that continues today.

social gaiety of the early amusement parks to social control. While Steeplechase promoted the apotheosis of the couple and the value of random strangers meeting and frolicking, Disneyland emphasized the family as the basic unit of the theme park. Disney forged many of his theme park fantasies in correlation with his daughter and the overall frame of the family: amusements must be safe, clean and focused on the enjoyment of the family. As a result of this shift in the social machine many critics have charged that the theme park has lost its role as catalyst for social and personal exploration.

In 1907 Fred Thompson provided an interesting comparison between the parks of Coney Island and Europe, choosing Blackpool as the only amusement venue worthy of comparison in his mind: 'the nearest thing that I find to Coney Island is Blackpool . . . but it is a long way behind. It is stiff and solemn, and its buildings lack the other-world suggestiveness of our Coney Island erections. Coney Island is frankly devoted to fun, the fantastic, the gay, the grotesque.'[33] Of course, Blackpool would outlast all of the amusement parks of Coney Island, suggesting that it, in fact, has something that the Coney Island parks lacked. Thompson's statement provides an interesting comparative opportunity. Luna Park was certainly more themed than Blackpool, but Blackpool perhaps had something more authentic that it maintains to this day. Visiting Blackpool in the twenty-first century one sees sights similar to those Thompson would have seen in his day. Impressive roller coasters, troikas and traditional shows and concessions reflect an emphasis not on theming but on another order – an authentic one in which people coexist peacefully with the amusement ride but do not enter the conceptual and cognitive realm that is promoted in theme parks. Today the Pleasure Beach persists in striking contrast with other theme parks throughout the United

Kingdom. It is the only park in the world, save Kennywood in Pennsylvania, that has one of the famed Noah's Ark rides. In stark contrast to Disney's perfected robots, this ride features mannequins like Noah and his bestiary of animals. Gags like a rocking boat are complemented by recreations of the Great Flood, a storm at sea and rooms of animals. Blackpool's use of Noah's Ark is historic. While the ride may not be as thrilling as the latest multi-million dollar simulation movie ride, it proves that public amusement has a history. Like this famous ride, the other attractions of Blackpool give a critique of the popular theme park trend.

As Thompson suggested many years ago, a park's 'other-world suggestiveness' has a direct bearing on the experiences of the patron. In the case of Blackpool there is no explicit theming; instead historic rides, historical plaques and dioramas featuring former park owners and managers provide an amusement order that is decidedly anti-thematic and anti-corporate. The 'stiff and solemn' nature of the park referenced in Thompson's interpretations might find a point of agreement with contemporary

The Noah's Ark ride – more than a ride since it combined musical elements and amusement ride techniques in one space.

amusement visitors, but another group, entirely hooked on the machine, would respond differently. For these people the machine, not the theme, the corporate logo, the movie-themed ride or stunt show, provides the only amusement truth. Many fans of Blackpool appreciate the park's historic rides, which have achieved the level of works of art: the Big Dipper, Grand National, Noah's Ark, Flying Machines. Such anti-theme park individuals who revere the machine and who eschew the corporatizing trends infecting the theme park share a kinship with 'ride junkies', individuals who cannot get enough of a ride. While working at AstroWorld I learned of a curious fellow known as Flumie. Flumie had ridden the park's log flume ride hundreds of times and I discovered that some workers I trained had a strange affinity with this man, some even calling him the park's most famous celebrity. Flumie proves that even inside theme parks, the machine can take prominence and can imbue an everyday individual like Flumie with serious social capital.

As contemporary Blackpool illustrates, one of the interesting facets of the amusement to theme park evolution is the presence of throwback or atavistic amusement parks in the era of theme parks. While Disney, Six Flags and Universal theme parks have influenced this new form of themed public amusement, some traditional parks have maintained their own identity, a different vision of amusement that snubs its nose at a form that has sometimes been called sanitized popular amusement. Like Blackpool Kennywood resolutely stands as an amusement park in an era of theme parks. The park, founded in 1898, sits outside Pittsburgh, in West Mifflin, Pennsylvania. It is a unique park in that it does not aspire to offer themed attractions and it allows people to bring in outside concessions. The park's website advertises it as a 'traditional amusement park' and 'historic landmark', suggesting a construction of identity in contrast to the contemporary theme park.[34] Kennywood's Lost Kennywood section pays homage to early parks, including the Luna parks of the east coast. Included in this section's design is a Shoot-the-Chutes that mimics the prominent architectural design of early Coney Island parks. The section also includes a strange site – a wall of homage to the early amusement parks of the east coast. Kennywood's motto 'Make a New Memory' emphasizes a contrast with the theme park's present-focused approach. Whereas Disneyland, the Magic Kingdom and Epcot celebrate the present and the future and offer the past only as simulacra, parks like Kennywood pay tribute to the past and offer telling reflection on the contemporary themed space.

The amusement park, like the theme park, is composed of machines – functional, robotic and conceptual. In the amusement park the machine is of utmost value since it is the device that contacts the patron's body in a direct sense. In the modern theme park the corporeal machines of blowing air and frenzied collisions, of the sort that populated Tilyou's Steeplechase, are minimized. The effects of amusements on the body, though still significant in the theme park, are lessened in favour of effects on the mind. Machines are used only as they can be themed and deployed as conceptual tools to connect people to the greater theme park narrative. The machine gives the theme park an important foundation that it must build on in order for it to persist, but the ways that it uses the machine are strikingly different, as Blackpool and Kennywood help emphasize. As the machine is further melded into the thematic landscapes of the contemporary theme park its greatest use is as a part of the larger symbolic order that is narrative: the story.

4 Theme Park as Show

Every man and woman should . . . play the noblest games and be of
another mind from what they are at present.
Plato[1]

In 1903 something new befell the amusement park. A noted inven-
tor of the infant incubator and reputable doctor named Martin A.
Couney presented the public with a scene the likes of which had not
been seen before – live human babies. People would come to view
Couney's infant incubators and gawk at the tiny children who were
but one part of the amusement spectacle at Coney Island.[2] Nearby,
the drama of fire-fighting, the dramatic reenactments of dark rides
like the Galveston Flood, and numerous aerial shows, animal pa-
geants and human ethnological freak shows offered the everyday
person an overall scene that was not available in books, in cinema
or in most forms of travel. Instead of having to travel to an exotic
country to see people and sights of a radically different nature, the
amusement park visitor only had to enter the gates of the Coney
Island amusement parks and travel in a virtual sense. The shows of
Coney were not fleeting moments of performance, as is often the
case in the contemporary consumer world; rather they sustained
something in people, some desire to be elsewhere, to be confronted with different experiences and to ultimately change the self. The
shows that emerged in the amusement parks of Coney, as well as in
the world's fairs, would later be transformed by the likes of the
theme park. Unlike the theme park as ride – in which the patron is
thrown by a ride but does not really interact with it – in the theme

park as performance, a key moment emerges: the individual is not simply watching leisure activities, he is a part of them. What pleasure gardens predicted was the desire of people to fully partake in their amusements. In the case of entertainment that evolved conterminously with the amusement park, including theatre and vaudeville, there is a distinction between the entertainment and the audience. In the case of Coney Island and its massive crowds a different narrative emerges, one of immersion in which 'audience and activity frequently merged'.[3]

The immersion effects of Coney Island suggested a form of total work – nothing short of a new world, unlike the one that the patron leaves behind, is created. Just as children play house in order to test the social roles expected of them later in life, amusement park patrons used the new world of Coney Island to suspend

Dr Martin A. Couney next to his famous infant incubators at Luna Park.

Joseph Pennell, 'The circus show at Luna Park', c. 1906.

their lives and take part in new ones, made possible by the combined effects of architecture, performance, rides and technology. Johan Huizinga wrote, 'Play . . . is of a higher order than seriousness. For seriousness seeks to exclude play, whereas play can very well include seriousness.'[4] And, as Roger Caillois says, play is total, a combination of all social, psychological and physical modes, and especially so when occurring within amusement parks.[5] Play of the sort at Coney Island introduced a new form of performance – one that was place-based (and thus corporeal) as opposed to ones that were mind-based (such as cinema and literature). Fantasy, in its fullest, must be given a place and this place, in turn, is asked to perform. As ushered in at the early amusement parks, the theme park form as play constitutes one of the most involved forms of popular performance.

The use of architecture in the theme park is paramount, but while the fabulous buildings of Coney Island amusement parks and the branded surreal structures of the world's fairs provided distinguishing features that were necessary to attract the patron's interest, it was not enough. In the 1960s architecture, along with theme parks, embarked on a path in which the building emerges from its functional identity and takes on a more symbolic one. In their influential book, *Learning from Las Vegas*, Venturi, Scott Brown and Izenour suggest a new agenda for architecture.[6] Taking cues from the popular, the spectacular and the symbolic, architecture moves from the industrial vernacular to the consumer vernacular.[7] The theme park, as it fully embodies the consumer vernacular and later passes it on to the themed space, including the casino, helps emphasize an architecture that, contra Ludwig Mies van der Rohe, is not a 'less is more' aesthetic but a 'more is more' one. While modernist Mies emphasized an austere style that highlighted function, the new architecture of the

theme park abandoned subtlety and form for impression and symbolism. When form did exist, it always lurked under the surface, disguised with the aesthetic and technological effects of theming. In short, the architecture of the theme park, as it developed from the maddening eclecticism of Fred Thompson's Luna Park, became an architecture in which performance was the primary effect.

Architecture always shows, but in the case of the theme park the showing is its primary function. In the spaces of Busch Gardens Europe, located in Williamsburg, Virginia, architecture illustrates its significant role in telling a story. Throughout the park the cultural ideals of the world – England, Scotland, Ireland,

'Gardens in Italy' at Busch Gardens Europe; within the theme park one can be in multiple places at once.

Italy, Germany, France and Canada – are represented in numerous foods, performances of dancers and singers, themed rides and many shops that sell goods related to each of the national ideals. Like Dollywood authenticity is emphasized at the European-themed park but, more than Dollywood, Busch Gardens Europe stresses architecture as its own performance. At the Banbury Cross theme land, the iconic Clock Tower of the Palace of Westminster (Big Ben) is re-created for theme park patrons who may never travel to London. In Killarney (Ireland), which was formerly themed as Hastings, England, patrons can board a simulator ride that replicates Irish mythology in miniature, or take up an Irish dancing show, all the while surrounded by quaint Irish towns of the past. In the park's two Italian themed areas, people can view Roman columns amid carefully manicured gardens. In Germany, Das Festhaus, which seats 2,000 people, immediately communicates with its iconic structure. Essentially, it says, within this space you can enjoy an 'oompah-style' band, watch German dancers and consume food and drink that represents what the building contains. Of course, the performance of architecture, like all performance, is based on a definitive crime against reality: certain symbolic features, some lifted from actual places and some imagined, become the representations used in performative architecture. As Wayne Curtis remarked, the authentic is 'something that looks as you imagine it might'.[8] In a sense it is an architecture of the 'perfect crime', as Baudrillard would say, in which the murder of reality is accomplished without 'the perpetrators, and the corpse of the real itself has never been found'.[9]

Busch Gardens Europe is a unique theme park in that it concentrates on European nations. The origins of performative architecture, however, pre-date this park. Beginning with

Disneyland, architecture as performance creates a legacy in all theme parks that would follow. The iconic Cinderella Castle and the homey Main Street USA become emblems for architecture's new role as conveyor of story. With Disney's entry into the theme park world, there is a new emphasis on the building and facade functioning as a primary caretaker in the narratives of theming found throughout a park. Cinderella Castle is a fabricated building that does more than any functional space can – while at Disneyland Resort Paris, I witnessed numerous people reduced to tears upon sight of the castle. While walking with people, including a former Disney worker, I was surprised and humbled that something as often dismissed as the theme park could play such a meaningful function in a person's life. During the visit, I recall speaking with the worker about some flaws that I noted at the park, including cleanliness. His

A sense of jolly Olde England is brought to life at Busch Gardens Europe.

silence and seeming disapproval was met with my decision to avoid any further such references to the park's problems. It seemed that Disneyland Resort Paris, much like a religious figure, a sacred icon or a place of worship, could not be the subject of the same criticisms that are often applied to other forms of culture. Such a moment, like a moment in which one is brought to tears while watching an amazing theatrical production or opera, illustrates the transformation that occurred as amusement parks moved beyond being places of the fantastic or even the sublime. The new theme park achieves the ultimate performance in that it convinces the patron, and often the worker, that architecture (and its varied stories) can have deep, personal and lasting meanings. Theme park architecture is no longer merely a form of representation, it is you – the most intimate of all cultural possibilities.

Only in rare moments, such on the opening day of the roller coaster Apollo's Chariot at Busch Gardens Europe, does the facade of theming and performance momentarily break down. Famous fashion model Fabio is one of the guests of honour, but the publicity event is spoiled as a goose hits Fabio in the face, breaking his nose and killing itself in the process. The poetic Apollo gives way in this moment of the real. Fabio said, following the mishap with the goose, that the park should implement measures to make sure that it never happens again. The performance, and the facade, break down; the Apollonian gives way to the Dionysian. Incidents like these, and more serious injuries, even deaths, momentarily affect the performance that is made possible by architecture and its integrated use of theming. Like Roland Barthes' punctum, reality peeks through, stings and cuts a hole through the facade of theming.[10] Even with such moments, themed architecture, in large part due to its ubiquitous role in consumer society, constantly revives and reinvents itself. Its culmination is Imagineering.

Imagineering, a form of material storytelling, fuses Walt Disney's efforts in animation, the ideologies of the day (the family, country, small towns and so on) with architecture, technology (including robots) and interior design. The effect is one that helped transform the theme park into an effective story.

An official Disney Imagineering text offers that

> Imagineered buildings are not simple structures or studio facades, but whole events. They are the illustrated book covers leading to the stories that await inside. Creating a sense of time, place and mood, Imagineered architecture can, in a single instant, transport you to a distant land.[11]

In Disney's advances in Imagineering there is a new emphasis on the story as a performative telling of place, event or idea in the world. A building can no longer be a functional space (the factory), and it can no longer be an avant-garde one (the Coney Island amusement park), it must now become a story in and of itself, and it must be used in decisive ways to connect to the real lives of people who visit theme parks. Whatever the associations might be with people – a sense of family, a sense of country, a sense of the good life, a sense of thrill – these must be worked into the structures of the buildings and facades of the theme park. In turn, these structures must be mobile – they must be deployed in imaginative ways and they must change as they interact with patrons. In short, they must wane like life itself and, ultimately, they must be playful in their various narratives of the world.

One of the greatest shows that the theme park shares a kinship with is the circus – specifically, the use of the animal. Back at Coney Island, one of the most interesting animal spectacles took place at Luna Park in 1903. Topsy was a famous performer elephant that eventually grew tired of the constant demand of entertaining people, and the disgruntled pachyderm took out her aggression on some of her handlers, reportedly killing three of them. Park management devised strategies for killing her, but this wasn't enough. A decision was made to involve Topsy in the greater spectacle of the amusement park. Poisoned carrots did not do the trick, and eventually the park set up a public electrocution of Topsy that was recorded for prosperity by Thomas Edison. In Luna's official programme, it is stated that 'Topsy was the first elephant in the world to be electrocuted' and in a world record time of one minute.[12] The spectacle, gruesome as it was, typified the ways in which animals would be used as entertainment at both the amusement and the theme park. Animals that resist the transformation of nature that is characterized by the amusement park are dealt with harshly. Like

The thrilling mysteries of animals were displayed for the many visitors to Coney Island.

the landscapes that theme parks contort into various shapes and appearances, animals are made into unnatural acts of performance.

Paul Boyton had the first inspiration to use the animal – the seal, lion, wolf – as a way of connecting with people. At the time watching performing seals and fierce lions in cages must have been amazing. Like the spectacles involving animals today, the fact that animals are unpredictable – consider the death of killer whale Kandu V at SeaWorld and the tiger attack on Roy Horn of the popular Siegfried & Roy show of the Mirage in Las Vegas – leads to the added value of the amusement. Though animal shows are in theory controlled, an animal can never be fully part of a show ensemble. The animal, like the nature that the theme park imposes itself upon, often strikes back in unpredictable ways.[13]

The difference between these uses of the animal and those of zoos, petting zoos and farms for families is that the theme park often uses the animal as both a form of spectacle and a means of theming. At Disney's Animal Kingdom spaces are themed around nature, and even though they are fabricated – including the creation of landscape features that provide people optimal viewing angles of animals, invisible berms that prevent carnivores from devouring smaller animals, and camouflaged logs and other natural features that hide feeding areas and are designed to lure the animal performers closer to the viewing areas of passing patrons on savannah rides – they contain numerous real plant and animal species. At night, animals, much like human performers, march back to their quarters (known as night houses). They are led by their trainers who use whistles and bells to request their evening return so they will not get in the way of gardeners who work diligently at night. Even the park's bats have been trained to perform on cue.

Early in his career, Walt Disney saw the value of the animal, especially in animation. During work on the animated classic *Bambi*,

Walt Disney requested that live deer be brought into his studio so that he could analyse their every movement.[14] It is said that Walt Disney 'felt that animals offered tremendous character studies' (they were inherently performative), and his attention to the movements and behaviours of real animals led to robotic approximations of them, like the Enchanted Tiki Room with its singing island birds.[15] Disney's desire was to appropriate, control and improve upon nature, first through animation and later through theme park technologies. While an architectural structure, such as the recreated Matterhorn at Disneyland, can be criticized as fabricated, it is difficult to argue with nature in its raw, moving and entertaining form. As Disney's official field guide to its Animal Kingdom theme park offers, 'There is nothing more real than these animals – they eat, sleep, hide, sleep, eat, and sleep some more (largely beyond our control). This reality permeated every facet of our design process.'[16]

The whale, along with other marine animals, is a powerful spectacle for many contemporary theme parks.

Much like Paul Boyton's animal performances at Sea Lion Park, SeaWorld does not use the animal merely as a backdrop for its setting and theme, but employs it as a performative truth. SeaWorld uses the powerful symbolic associations of the killer whale to connect patrons with performing animals. As Susan G. Davis argues, the effect is a powerful corporate one that utilizes nature in the service of culture.[17] SeaWorld has been the subject of protests by animal rights activists, and the study of an extensive expose by PBS *Frontline*.[18] Many have complained about the cruel process that leads to the capture of such animals and the later captive life that is dedicated to the entertaining of humans in theme parks. The animal shows at theme parks give a glimpse of another reality – the wild one that is typically out of view of the experiences of the everyday customer. Parks like Animal Kingdom and SeaWorld suggest that they only show people what animals are really like, but as is the case with any recreation in a

The visitor is always caught up in a crowd; like being in society itself, the individual is made aware of others and must move in relation to them.

theme park, what is shown to people is nature copied, reframed and filtered for an era of popular consumption. Many theme parks, including Dollywood and Busch Gardens, use animals as a means of stressing conservation with patrons. While it is debatable that theme parks can lay claim to conservation – they are, after all, spaces of culture imposed upon nature – they use the idea of conservation and the symbolic associations of animals to powerful performative effect.

In order for a theme park patron to be present in a park – that is, conscious – she must be made a participant in all that unravels around her. Interestingly, this concept emerges much sooner than the late 1950s with Disneyland. In fact, during a trip to the World's Columbian Exposition, Frederick Law Olmsted found the atmosphere to be surprisingly convivial, if not too 'melancholy' and contemplative.[19] What the space needed was gaiety and thus Olmsted suggested to Daniel Burnham the addition of performers from the festival

The Virginia Reel, like many other attractions at Coney Island, established a tradition of visitors entertaining themselves.

Midway inside the rest of the White City.[20] The principle of constant activity as a part of entertainment – as something that will envelop the patron at each and every turn – is picked up by the amusement park at Coney Island. For performance to supplant reality it must achieve absolute meaning in the patron. It is a form of catharsis, as Aristotle wrote of drama, in which emotions are purified by vicarious experience.[21] Activity of varied sorts, and the involvement of the patron in all of it, is at the heart of Olmsted's concerns about the melancholy nature of the Columbian Exposition.

At Coney Island a similar move was afoot to bring the park patron into closer proximity with the amusements. Asking a patron to be motivated to ride a ride or enter a fun house is not sufficient, and at Luna Park Fred Thompson had performance in mind when he set out to activate people as the nodes of his architectural dreamscape. So determined was Thompson to involve his patrons in his spectacles that 'when people sat down Thompson would immediately dispatch a band of musicians to the scene in an attempt to rouse his customers' spirits and thus bring them to their feet'.[22] In this way Luna Park set a powerful precedent that would be followed at other theme parks, especially Six Flags and Disney. What Thompson realized was something revolutionary – that people would not be satisfied by simply watching the spectacle of the amusement park and solemnly taking it all in, such as one might experience on a nature hike; rather, the patron must be motivated by symbolic forces. He or she must be given a reason to throw aside the moral orders of the society that are placed on hold while in the park. An individual associated with the famous Macy's Thanksgiving Day Parade said that 'a spectacle lifts you up and takes you into vastness. It makes you feel expansive, like you are greater than you.'[23] Even more profound than the kinetic thrills of the ride is the cognitive and existential thrill of feeling that one

is part of something – a narrative of inclusion that approaches the ideals of religion and the intimacy of kinship.

At theme parks like the Holy Land Experience in Orlando, Florida, there is an even deeper connection made between the experiences of the customer and the themes developed in the amusement venue. The constant activity and the involvement of the patron that was Thompson's dream is connected to a more profound aspect of the customer. It is the world of the customer, located outside the confines of the theme park, that is used, modified and refocused. Walking into the gates of the Holy Land, the guest is greeted with the welcoming of 'Shalom'. A path down the old streets of Jerusalem, complete with costumed performers and souvenir ships, leads people to a number of the park's attractions, including The Scriptorium: Center for Biblical Antiquities, which

Jesus carrying his cross at The Holy Land Experience.

houses historic Bibles and presents or performs the history of the Bible using technology, museum-like displays and music and lighting techniques. At the end of the Scriptorium and a dramatic Ten Commandments room, patrons exit through a typical room, complete with computers, a television and all the conveniences of the home. They are then given a powerful message as they are asked, 'What are you doing'? A voice, perhaps of God, asks participants to reflect on their own religiosity and thus the performance of the Scriptorium (in which Bibles take on an immaterial existence) is attached to the lifeworld of the visitor. The park uses simulation that transports people back to the ancient times of the Bible and then shocks them back to reality by simulating an everyday space that looks surprisingly like that of the outside world. The effect often leads guests to tears, and helps emphasize the unique ways in

The Scriptorium: Center for Biblical Antiquities (at The Holy Land Experience).

which a theme park can combine architecture, interior design, dramatic illustration and technology to produce an overall performative power that is almost entirely inward-directed.

At the Holy Land Experience performance is used not simply as a means of connecting patrons to the overall narrative of the park, it also forms an important technique of social control. Since the amusement parks of Coney Island, a major problem has been the control of amusement populations. All theme parks, by their nature, invite large numbers of people to their spaces. The crowd is a tradeoff for expensive attractions, and no theme park can be successful without attracting large numbers of people. The difficulty lies in how to manage crowds in two senses: the first, moving the sheer numbers of people through the park in an efficient way, and the second, discussed in the next chapter, assuring that people act in appropriate ways. Neither is an easy task.

Since amusement parks became enclosed spaces – most notably at Steeplechase Park – they have proclaimed a powerful mastery over space. They defined themselves apart from the rest of the world, and eventually this spatial distinction would lead to a branding distinction that is found in the modern theme park. By enclosing itself from the outside Steeplechase emphasized a unique vision of the world and provided unity, unlike a carnival or state fair in which disorganized attractions and amusement juxtapositions suggested disunity. And this unity provided the amusement park with the unique task of controlling the populations that entered its spaces. Contemporary theme parks have increased their attention to the precise control of people. Because rides, shows and performances last different time periods, and because patrons can spend time in uncontrolled ways, such as eating lunch, it is important that the theme park manage the timing and scheduling of a patron's experience, with the caveat that this management not be noticed by people. This sort of overall holistic performance conceals its intentions, and it is so effective in its means that it allows the theme park to spread. As it does, it even exceeds itself and soon becomes a form that is unseen and unnoticed – an invisible theme park.

Rides and shows are one of the primary means by which populations are managed within the theme park. In contemporary theme parks careful attention is given to expanding the thematic vistas of the landscape to as many sectors of the map as possible. As people move along, their eyes and other senses participate in an elaborate unfolding story. And when they board a ride, the experience and, most importantly, the time is controlled to precision. In some theme parks, including the Chinese Ethnic Culture Park in Beijing and the Holy Land Experience, there is a further addition of precision: people are told the order in which to experience the theme park's pleasures, and thus an even larger (time) unit of their lives is managed by the park. At the Chinese Ethnic Culture Park pacing is used to move people through the park in an orderly fashion and helps 'naturalize the visitors' consciousness for consumption'.[24] At the Holy Land schedules given to patrons upon entrance to the park describe the times at which certain activities may be visited, and park workers, including those in gift shops, advise people on when they should see certain attractions.

While patrons can be controlled in terms of the timing and pacing of their experiences, a simple fact confronts the theme park: the line. The queue line is not unique to the theme park but may be associated with consumer society in general. On the Internet, websites like the British Standinaqueue reflect the uniquely human affliction of the line.[25] People wait in line to purchase goods or food or to visit popular attractions. On the Internet virtual queue lines have sprung up as people wait to buy concert

tickets and other consumable items. Within the theme park, the queue line serves the same function as other lines outside theme parks – purchasing food and souvenirs, and waiting to see a show or ride a ride – but the theme park line can be typically longer than other lines, and thus the theme park must devise a performative strategy to deal with the problem of the line. After all, why would people choose to wait up to three hours in a line, especially on a hot summer day, just to get on a ride that lasts only a few minutes?

One strategy, often employed at Disney theme parks, is to hide lines. Using design techniques, lines shoot out in unknown directions, and just when people believe that they have made it to the ride boarding area, they realize they are not there yet.[26] This technique creates a show of the process of waiting in line. As people queue 'new friendships are continually renewed' and people begin to talk to one another, exchanging experiences and stories in a gregarious event.[27] This natural social performance helps make the line waiting more bearable, but theming and sensory technologies

In order to enjoy a theme park, one must first wait in line.

are even more powerful ways of controlling queues. Line areas are typically themed in accord with the attraction, and this may include sounds from speakers and video screens, foliage and landscaping, and other components that heighten the experience of waiting in line. These approaches create an instance of Freud's pleasure principle in which people are told that the wait will be worth it. Like the progression of cinema, queue line effects and theming help develop the story, and as people approach the ride and are ready to board it, they have already physically and cognitively moved through much of the story that the ride will complete. Queue lines, through their theming, help perform and thus entertain patrons as they wait for the main attraction but, most importantly, people, as they are drawn into the narrative of the attractions, help deliver the performance themselves.[28]

Thematic architecture can only go so far in conveying the illusion of place, fantasy and the break from the everyday, and asking

At the Festhaus at Busch Gardens Europe, patrons feast on traditional German fare and experience the sensory thrills of the Oompah Band and Festhaus dancers, celebrating Oktoberfest throughout the season.

patrons to get involved in live drama could be a difficult task, for people are naturally fickle. A more profound equalizer is needed – one that like animals gave life and movement to the dramas. Namely, people act as performers. Many theme parks, like the amusement parks of the past, use the stage performance as a means of connecting people with the theme or amusements of the park as well as elevating the overall symbolic importance of the theme park. Stage performances provide patrons with needed respite between rides and eating and importantly act as variety that helps establish a day in a theme park as an overall experience. In addition to stage performances, all workers, in one way or another, are asked to perform for patrons.

Theme parks, as contemporary conveyors of powerful spectacles, are effective precisely because they eliminate the seams that characterize the 'seedy' spaces of the past, including amusement parks and carnivals. When one boards a carnival ride and is confronted

At Universal Studios Japan, the ready-made story of Peter Pan is used to create a pyrotechnic, live-action show for patrons.

by a surly ride worker – complete with tattoos and ragged street clothes – the person can only experience the ride. Nothing is beyond it – it is the only truth of the space. In a theme park the worker is costumed, he does not merely operate the ride, and he uses his abilities as a performer to extend the ride in two ways. First, he performs a themed role in the space – one that is consistent with the mood of the ride or venue. At AstroWorld, for example, workers at the Greezed Lightnin' were expected to wear their costumes correctly and deliver a meaningful speech or performance (a spiel) that was themed in a way consistent with the Western focus of the area. In this case theming 'is not merely an architectural technology of the material world; it is a means of social interaction, a performative practice, and even an existential state that is dually manifested by workers and patrons at themed venues'.[29] Second, the worker performs a transitional role. As a performer he can show the patron a

The Curse of DarKastle at Busch Gardens Europe: while aboard, riders experience the simultaneous thrill of ride propulsion, 3D digital media, and special effects.

good time and then suggest other things that the patron can do in another theme land. The effect is cinematic, with actors helping create the edits between theme lands. As one Imagineer suggested, the roots of Disney theme parks are in movies: 'the idea that visitors who stepped into this new park should feel as though they stepped into a movie. Every inch of the place should be part of a story, as in a movie or television show.'[30]

Unfortunately, performance is a precarious thing, and people often forget that controlling workers as they play out their roles, even at Disney theme parks, is never easy. Years ago when a young boy at Disneyland's Tom Sawyer Island was asked to play the part of Tom Sawyer he took the role (that he had learned about in Mark Twain's *The Adventures of Tom Sawyer*) so seriously that he acted aggressively to patrons and even started fist fights with other boys who visited the island.[31] What this incident suggests is that people will bring their own attitudes to the roles that they play – just as actors would on a stage – so it is incumbent on the contemporary theme park to apply more pressure on the worker. Just as the caged animals of Sea Lion Park could never be fully trusted, the theme park worker must be watched

A designer at Universal Orlando works on an important part of the performative materials of the theme park.

carefully. Most importantly, performative behaviours must be managed and tuned in accord with the philosophy of the particular theme park.

Workers must be watched at all times – part of my profession as a theme park trainer – and this includes secret undercover audits in which the theme park trainer performs as a patron would. In some cases she might attempt to do something out of the ordinary just to check the abilities of the worker and the park's organizational system. Undercover audits of this sort have a major bearing on the theme park worker. In theme park training programmes further performances are used to stimulate the effective worker. Role-playing, improvisation and scenarios are deployed by trainers in an attempt to predict situations that they might encounter with real people out in the parks. Many contemporary theme parks have expanded and refined the original foci of the early amusement parks, particularly in the ways in which they have expanded performance from the stages of acrobats, circus performers and animals to a situation in which 'all the world's a stage'.

With Walt Disney's theme park ventures, the theme park takes on a new interpersonal dimension. Whereas in the past it was possible for customers to observe amusement park workers in naturalistic ways, the contemporary theme park utilizes a dramaturgical approach to the interpersonal. Disney's movie and entertainment background resulted in an ideology of the stage – workers became 'cast members', patrons became 'guests' and the entirety of the amusement park became a 'stage'. No longer were the interactions of patrons and workers everyday or normal; now each interaction was scripted, with the whole thing becoming a play or act. This move to dramaturgy was one of the most significant transformations in the evolution of the theme park. Other transformations were significant – such as the expansion of the capital used to create architecture, rides, and attractions – but this particular one was monumental because it affected the very nature of life within theme parks. Now people, just like architecture and geography, became exotic, scripted and performative. Dramaturgy, of the sort resulting from Disney and Six Flags theme parks and their use of 'staging', 'guests' and the like, has now moved well beyond the frontiers of theme parks. In everyday life businesses use Disney's theatrical methods to condition their own practices and presumably increase their profits, while city planners devise architectural ways to achieve a utopian vision of order that even Olmsted could not fully realize in Central Park. The result is a 'world theme park' of scripted interactions, predetermined emotions and predictable outcomes.

Of course there is a history of inequality in the evolutionary track of the theme park. The earliest amusement parks and world expositions, as much as they offered a democratic opportunity for people to share in the same amusements, were often marked by racialism, segregation and exclusionary rules. Even Disney's theme parks made distinctions: a certain type of worker was desirable, and a specific class of patron was similarly sought. As the theme park has evolved, the careful scripting of social interactions, the use of dramaturgy to affect social life, and the development of mechanisms that seek to civilize worker and patron have expanded simultaneously.[32] Within contemporary quasi-theme park spaces, such as fantasy shopping malls, themed restaurants and casinos, much of the dramaturgical legacy of Disney and Six Flags theme parks can be found. The ideology that 'guest is always right' has extended to many service spaces of contemporary life. When these spaces are themed the ideology is even more at play because the assumption is that the people playing roles (workers) and the people receiving them (patrons) are all a part

of the scene or the stage. In a general sense, quotidian aspects of the space – most notably the exchanges of commodities and services – become secondary to the drama and role playing which eventually surpasses the functional uses of the space.

The scripting of the theme park as a stage begins with Disney's vision of a more wholesome theme park space. The unsavoury nature of early amusement parks, with their carnie-like employees, rude social interactions and run-down environs, is replaced by sanitized, predetermined and seamless interactions. Just like architecture that is cleaned up, as Paul Goldberger once said, Disney 'corrects all the mistakes' and re-presents a new social form.[33] Later

Signal Three (Thad Donovan); here, the theme park, as an object of human fears and desires, takes on a new representation.

Six Flags picked up on the ideology of Disney. In fact, in the 1990s the corporation hired a former Disney corporate trainer to instil Disney-like 'culture' into Six Flags theme parks, and the result was numerous campaigns like 'Guest First' and 'Gold Standard' that aimed to achieve a more pristine service culture.

One of the results of these efforts to turn the theme park into a site of dramaturgy is an obsession with the backstage. Within the evolutionary track of the object, just as space within the theme park is zoned according to theme and function, the overall social space of interactions is zoned into the front stage and the backstage. The front is the space that is part of the 'magic', in Disney terms, or that which includes the fantasy as it is intended to be seen, while the back is the space that is off limits to the experience of the patron. In 1989, it is reported, Disney settled a lawsuit with a family whose daughters experienced the sight of a Disney cartoon character without its head on. One of the daughters apparently

As was also the practice at numerous world's fairs, here at Dreamland Igorots are on display.

needed psychiatric treatment as a result of 'nightmares that she was being chased by headless giants'.[34] In that moment, as in the accident involving Fabio and the goose, the artifice of the theme park collides with the realism of everyday life, and at that moment the front and the backstages enter into opposition. Such incidents, and there have been numerous similar ones, put pressure on the theme park to deliver perfect entertainment, and also place emphasis on the patron to experience a theme park without sutures. Within the United States and the United Kingdom television shows focused on themed and service spaces – including *Welcome to the Parker, American Casino, Airport, Luton Airport* and *Caesars 24/7* – illustrate how fascinating behind-the-scenes spaces are.[35] Ironically for the theme park, though the emphasis on the overall experience is a dramaturgical one, at the same time such staging creates a desire in the customer to get behind the scenes and perhaps discover, as did the little girl, the dark side of the theme park.[36]

Samuel Gumpertz, the creator of the famed Lilliputia at Dreamland, once said that 'The only way to make an old show go is to hang out a new sign – and that won't work more than one time with the audience.'[37] Gumpertz would eventually become Dreamland's general manager and then end his career with Ringling Brothers circus. For Gumpertz the odd performed: whether Igorots imported from the Philippines, or the small people of Lilliputia, or constant circus performances in the centre of Dreamland, or human oddities/freak shows, he understood the power of bringing the surreal to the amusement park and asking it to act. Of course, Gumpertz' project was anti-intellectual; there was no emphasis on using these various performances to teach people anything, other than that they were higher than others in a physical or evolutionary sense. The oddities of the world were presented to the amusement park patron to both shock and reassure.

At today's theme park explicit racialism and human oddities have been eliminated in favour of more wholesome attractions. Contemporary living heritage spaces, including Colonial Williamsburg in Virginia; Cosmeston Medieval Village near Cardiff; Conner Prairie in Indiana; Plimoth Plantation in Massachusetts; the Polynesian Cultural Center in Hawaii; and Shakaland in South Africa use historical reenactments and cultural performances in ways reminiscent of theme parks. While it is debatable whether these places are theme parks – they are smaller in scale and lack notable amusement rides – they clearly use exoticism as a form of entertainment that has become a staple of the theme park industry. Such places promise an authentic historical or cultural experience by immersing visitors in the sights, smells, tastes and bodily experiences of a culture that has been re-created for the purposes of entertainment, but a debate emerges, can theme parks then educate the public?

Though not a theme park, the Polynesian Cultural Center uses theme park approaches – including architectural recreations, performance and authenticity – to create a theme park-like experience.

Inside the hybrid world of Dickens World at Chatham, Kent, literary characters are brought to life and visitors can do more than experience literature in the mind; they can walk through it in space.

Just as the line between education and entertainment has blurred, so too have the lines between theme parks, museums, heritage sites and other venues. In the contemporary world the theme park competes with the museum for relevance – often stating that it is making a difference by teaching people something important, not just entertaining them. For the museum, competition with popular culture requires that it present its educational displays using forms of technology, interior design and interactive dioramas that appear surprisingly like those in theme parks. Many contemporary spaces that could be read as theme parks, in part due to their use of performance as a means of staging a past place or event, avoid the label of theme park since it might detract from their efforts at presenting a pedagogical lesson for customers. Such is the case of Dickens World in Kent, England.

Press releases from Dickens World state that it is a complex that is themed, but avoid explicit reference to the word 'theme park'. The park promises to take visitors back to the nineteenth-century world of Charles Dickens, whose work is familiar to many readers worldwide. Dickens World 'will take visitors on a journey of Dickens' lifetime as they step back in time to Dickensian England to experience the highs and lows of urban life complete with sounds and smells'.[38] The park includes a themed boat ride that transports riders back to the dingy world of London described in many of Dickens' works, actors who interact with patrons in the space, an Ebenezer Scrooge haunted house, and historical reconstructions like schoolhouses and jails. One of the most interesting spaces is Fagin's Den soft play area, named after the character Fagin from *Oliver Twist*, who made boys work for him as pickpockets. According to the venue's managing director, such contradictions are due to the park's emphasis on entertainment: 'Visitors are not going to come here to be depressed so our

role is to entertain them. We're not going to have starving babies crawling around on the cobblestones.'[39]

Because of the high culture associations of Charles Dickens, careful attention is given to what the park describes as 'a credible and factual account of Charles Dickens' works and the world in which he lived'.[40] Regardless of these efforts to substantiate the bringing to life of the Dickens literary world, some critics have complained that Dickens' literary work cannot be appreciated from a thematic and entertainment perspective, while others claim that the theme park reflects a way to connect with an increasingly media-saturated populace.[41] One blogger on the Internet said, 'Oh dear, sometimes the whole of Britain seems to be turning into one large theme park, and nobody seems sure where reality ends and fantasy begins.'[42] Of course, the other side of the argument is that Dickens World is doing something that is

At the Jorvik Viking Centre in York, education, archaeology, and theme park rides combine.

not possible with high culture – using the performative associations of Charles Dickens, however diluted, to increase interest in one of the world's great writers.

Edwin Slosson, describing the recreated amusements of Coney Island, including the Galveston Flood and other reenactments, said, 'Considered as spectacles some of these are very ingeniously given, and since they are accompanied by a lecture, they have some educational value.'[43] Slosson was perhaps on to something in that he recognized the partial educational value of amusement parks. In today's world more venues employ theme park-like technologies, forms of performance and other techniques to connect people to places, other people, cultures, historical periods and brands. As such, theme parks function as complex cultural conveyors. They present a representation of another place, another culture, another time or mood in symbolic ways. Perhaps when the architectural representations of the theme park are conceived of as a dialogue instead of a monologue, as a fluid form rather than a solid structure, the theme park moves from hegemony to pedagogy. In this way it is possible to conceive of the theme park as a mediator between cultures. Venues like Jorvik Viking Centre in York, England, for example, use theme park approaches, including a Pirates of the Caribbean-style ride, to connect people with Viking archaeology and culture history. Were one to scoff at such an effort, it may be worth asking whether any harm is done in such an entertaining portrayal of serious archaeology and culture history if it sparks interest among people and furthers self-education?

The Strip of Las Vegas, a four-mile section of the city, has been labelled by many as an adult theme park. In identifying it as such, people suggest that there are theme park elements within the various places of the Las Vegas Strip. In the 1990s the concept of the theme park began to expand to include varying spaces such as

museums, restaurants and heritage centres, and the theme park became a global form. In its movement away from the United States and from the visions of Walt Disney, the theme park became something more. As the theme park connects with the brand, it alters its architecture, technology, design and use to fit the new world of branding, but maintains its emphasis on story, and even expands it to include a more pronounced connection with the identity of the patron. In multiple ways Vegas is the epitome of the theme park as a form. Thematic architecture, branding in the form of chain restaurants, logos and corporate signage, high energy rides, attractions and performances, and uses of decor, architecture and interior design that are incredibly evocative, all combine in an overall lifestyle, experience and affective construction that hits at the core of everyday people. In new forms of theming on the Strip and in numerous other spaces, the patron, as she completes the drama of what is unfolding around her, now forms a vital part of the foundation of new themed spaces.[44]

Public shows like the Sirens at Treasure Island (now T. I.) suggest an interesting adaptation of the theme park. Like the shows of

The Sirens at Treasure Island suggest a new possible meeting of the theme park and public sexuality.

Coney Island and those of Disney theme parks, the Sirens offers a performance that combines singing, dancing, humour, pyrotechnics and moving sets but, unlike earlier shows in amusement and theme parks, the Sirens is clearly adult oriented. Actresses in the performance make crude jokes aimed at adults, and the costuming and suggestive dancing looks nothing like the sanitized and chaste amusements of most theme parks. Moving through the Treasure Island one sees constant references to the pirate theme, including building features, signage and attractions of all sorts. On other parts of the Strip there are casinos that look like theme parks proper, including the Circus Circus, which interestingly divides adult spaces (like bars and casinos) off from child spaces (like the circus, rides and carnival games) using maps and colour coding. Such crude and functional divisions illustrate a tension that the theme

The view of the New York–New York Hotel and Casino; visual space itself becomes a theme park for the eyes.

park experiences. Las Vegas draws on the theme park's spectacular and eclectic architecture, its emphasis on varied entertainment and shows and its creation of a fully embodied world but, as it incorporates all of these tendencies in its casinos, it loses the enclosure that it gained from Steeplechase Park.[45] With the building of the next spectacular and iconic casino on the Strip, a greater theme park – what sometimes people refer to when they say, 'The Strip is a big theme park' – emerges. People do not just go to one of the casinos, their senses tell them to visit as many as possible, a Grand Tour in the realm of pop consumerism. Each casino acts as a quasi-theme park, while the whole becomes what can be called a mega-theme park. The world, in turn, picks up on the modes of delivery, the performances, the images, and seeks to transform itself into a world theme park. At some point it becomes

At Legoland California, the images of the Las Vegas Strip are recreated in a meta-moment of the theme park.

impossible to distinguish between the images, ideas and activities that are taking place within a theme park, and those that flash before our eyes on television screens and on the street.

The theme park is also unable to deal with the new adult-oriented focus of its amusements. Walt Disney created Disneyland with the image of his daughter in mind – he wanted to protect her from the world, not expose her to its often dangerous verities. He certainly would not approve of the direction that his amusements have taken in Las Vegas. But perhaps there is a movement back to the world of Coney Island, with its freak shows, electrocuted elephants, displays of people and absurdist entertainment. While Disneyland took the theme park into the realm of the Apollonian and the proper, Las Vegas perhaps moves it back to the Dadaistic and the Rabelaisian. As the theme park expands, it will continue to unfold in new and surprising spaces, even beyond those of Las Vegas. Theme parks institute new forms that maintain one primary element of the mould that emerged at Disneyland and Six Flags Over Texas: theming. With this moment, in which performance achieves its apogee in themed spaces, the theme park is ready to makes its final ascent. As it moves into even closer proximity with the individual, her lifeworld and all that she is, a holistic performance is launched, and it is one that is greater than the sum of architecture, theming, performance and park rides that it uses – it is the brand.

5 Theme Park as Brand

All that once was directly lived has become mere representation.
Guy Debord[1]

Responding to evangelist Billy Graham's description of his visit to
Disneyland as a 'nice fantasy', Walt offered that, 'You know the fantasy
isn't here. This is very real . . . The park is reality. The people are natural
here; they're having a good time; they're communicating. This is what
people really are. The fantasy is – out there, outside the gates of
Disneyland, where people have hatreds and people have prejudices.
It's not really real!'[2]

In the contemporary world the most significant transformation of
the theme park involves the brand. Whether the marks on the
casks of wine, the symbols placed on livestock for purposes of
identification or the modern (trade)marks on items, the brand is
something that is first literally burned on a thing and later is fig-
uratively burned into the consciousness.[3] Brands may include
corporate symbolism and ideology (such as Mickey Mouse), certain
experiences associated with a product (such as the relaxation of a
Starbucks cafe or the hominess of an REI outdoor sports store) or
even more generalizable qualities like those connected to a famous
celebrity. When used in conjunction with the right delivery device
the brand can provide stronger and more meaningful associations
between a consumer and the product. In particular, when the
brand in unleashed in space – as in the theme park – one of the
most potent connections can be made.

The first step towards the theme park as brand began at

Steeplechase Park. George Tilyou understood the need for a distinctive amusement place with which people could connect. Simply visiting a random place of amusement, such as a carnival, does not leave a profound effect on the customer; while he may be entertained, he is not transformed. What Tilyou accomplished was the creation of deeper and iconic associations between his amusement park and his patrons. The steeplechase horse ride was very popular in the United Kingdom and horse racing was a craze in the United States, so Tilyou used the icon of the steeplechase as a foundation for his amusement park. This branded his park as a unique and memorable place. The steeplechase established a symbolic connection between the park and the patron, while the park's enclosure helped distinguish itself from both the outside world and other parks. This seemingly simple fact – of using the berm to mark itself off like a nation would its borders – gave the theme park an impetus for its movement into the world of branding.

At new theme park spaces like Star Trek: The Experience (Las Vegas Hilton), people's science fiction fantasies are met in multiple ways.

A second facet that Tilyou introduced at Steeplechase was the memorable 'funny face'. The funny face became the symbol of Steeplechase for many years. It was iconic for its distorted and distinctive looks: an uncanny 44 teeth caused some passers-by on Surf Avenue to 'wince as they passed by'.[4] On postcards sent from the park, viewers could see the noticeable face – a playful image – that though generic created a clear association between Tilyou's park and those who visited it. The 'fun place', as Steeplechase dubbed itself, was connected with the image of the funny face. Later amusement parks, like Asbury Park in New Jersey, used a similar iconic image that came to be known as 'Tillie'.[5] Later Disney would employ the already popular Mickey Mouse character at Disneyland, while other parks, beginning in the 1980s, used cartoon characters, animals and products of all types to create the same symbolism that started with the funny face. For children,

George Tilyou's 'funny face' (top) created a memorable icon that theme parks would use to great success later.

A view of the crowds approaching the iconic Disneyland in Anaheim, California.

including those who were drawn to Disneyland Paris, their initial experiences with Disney cartoon characters were transferred to the immersive realm of theme parks.[6] In many Disney theme parks a popular pastime of patrons is to search for 'hidden Mickeys' – silhouettes of the famous corporate icon that are found in topiary features and on buildings and rides. In today's theme park the effect of such identification with corporate symbolism is startling. As some have said (and complained), today's theme park looks nothing like the amusement parks of old. Some have called Disney parks 'logoland' and other theme parks brandlands.[7] While Tilyou's Steeplechase did have a distinctive logo that undoubtedly contributed to the popularity of his amusement park, his logo was unlike the corporate logo of today, and his park was not a corporate theme park. Soon the logo would become recognizable (Mickey Mouse) and the form iconic (Disneyland), in no small part due to the synthesis of the logo and the form.

Like the United States Japan has been the site of some of the most compelling fusions of theme park and brand. In 2001 the Themed Entertainment Association named Kidzania (Kid's City International of Mexico) the top theme park in the world with its Thea Award. The honour is in no small part due to the uniqueness of Kidzania. Xavier López Ancona opened the first Kidzania in Mexico City and the concept was later picked up in Japan. This hybrid space is geared at children, who may choose from over 70 different professions – airline pilot, airline stewardess, restaurant worker, hospital attendant, car mechanic, photographer, parcel delivery person and many others. The aim of the park is to create what it calls 'edutainment', or the use of entertainment technologies to teach children about professions in the world. The aim seems very innocent – after all, what could be more harmless than teaching kids about real professions? The sinister side is found,

however, in the powerful branding connections that are established in all of the park's simulations. The airline simulations are connected with All Nippon Airways, the hospital ones with Johnson and Johnson, and the burger shop ones with MOS Burger, a Japanese fast-food chain. The overall effect, according to branding guru Martin Lindstrom, who incidentally lauds Kidzania, is that 'brands are having a very natural role here . . . almost like a replicant from the real life'.[8] Interestingly, while Kidzania attempts to teach children about the value of brands while inside a fun theme park, for one at least – a boy making hamburgers – the effect may have been lost: 'When asked what his favorite hamburger was, right after he finished his 30 minutes making MOS burgers, one 9-year-old boy instantly replied, "McDonald's!" Then he dashed off to get into the line to make pizzas.'[9]

Kidzania in Japan, a place where children can act like adults, if only for a day and if only through brands.

Walt Disney understood the powerful imprinting effect that brands can have on children. He said, 'I think of a child's mind as a blank book. During the first years of his life, much will be written on the pages. The quality of that writing will affect his life profoundly.'[10] Like all modern theme parks Kidzania uses the techniques of simulation and fantasy to remarkable effects. Its attractions are even more closely connected to the lifeworld of patrons, in this case children. Parents are allowed to watch from the sidelines, and children are given the reins of potential future careers, all as branded and natural forms. Traditional theme park rides often allow people to only partially escape from everyday reality. In this instance children are asked to participate fully in a miniaturized community, complete with currency (kidzos), ATMs and bank accounts.[11] Henry A. Giroux has called Disney a 'teaching machine' and, in the ways in which contemporary theme parks aim to achieve forms of 'edutainment', it can be maintained that theme parks have taken on new pedagogical functions in society, in some ways surpassing museums, the written word and even schools.[12]

What Kidzania helps establish is that theme parks have evolved from places of varied amusement, spectacular architecture and thrilling rides. They first become places, through the technology of theming, and second become branded places, accomplished by their entering into an intimate relationship with the corporation and its associated trappings – logos, ideologies, feelings, senses, experiences and myths. A key moment in the theme park, emphasized by venues like Kidzania, is when the theme park sheds its identity as a theme park. As the theme park evolves, it sheds its earlier status of acting only as a form of amusement and thrill; now, though it still aims to thrill patrons, it recognizes a more powerful role – that of altering society itself.

The tradition of combining brands with thematic architecture, technological displays and entertaining attractions begins at the world's fair. The exposition used the brand as a means of identifying a key technology or historical moment of a nation – the automobile, electricity, etc. – and then created an iconic association between the brand and the general thing being depicted. While visiting a world's fair, the patron undergoes a significant revelation: it is not that the person visiting an electricity display understands the principle of electricity, rather, he understands that electricity is associated with a specific company such as General Electric. As Umberto Eco wrote of the expo, 'the prestige game is won by the country that best tells what it does, independently of what it actually does'.[13] At the same time brands became more distinctive not simply through their display as functional items, but as symbolic ones. One of the primary ways in which the brand becomes materialized is through spectacular architecture. At the 1915 Panama-Pacific International Exposition in San Francisco a new ordinance forbade the use of signs or billboards. Facade

Panama-Pacific International Exposition: On the Zone.

architecture – in which 'each attraction became an advertisement of itself either in its three-dimensional form or by means of visual cues' – was the result.[14] Giant tin soldiers, a scale model of the Grand Canyon, a Blarney castle and a giant Buddha building created a zone of merchandized architecture that would affect future forms, including the franchise architecture now common in fast food restaurants like McDonalds and Taco Bell.

Brands are not simply introduced in theme parks, rather they have evolved with them, almost naturally. One of the significant ways in which such a connection is made and maintained is a clear result of the theme park's development as a civilizing form. In his design of Central Park Frederick Law Olmsted envisioned the famous park of New York City as more than a refuge from the urban chaos; it was a new form that could actually change people and promote temperance in society; '"rude, noisy fellows", as they entered the park, became "hushed, moderate and careful".'[15] All people could theoretically participate in the space, but they had to agree to being altered in the process. As Coney Island evolved from a lurid site of pickpockets, prostitutes, thieves, conmen and dead bodies washing up on the beaches, it became respectable. While the early amusement parks allowed for rebellion from the rules of everyday society, they did so at a price. By enclosing their spaces amusement parks notified the public that they controlled the amusement – in architectural, spatial and even psychological senses. One who becomes too unruly is escorted out, and the same phenomenon occurs in the contemporary quasi-theme parks of the Las Vegas Strip. In a corporate version of the social contract people relinquish control of themselves in exchange for gaiety, spectacles and entertainment that are impossible outside the theme park.

While working at Six Flags AstroWorld I became associated with the civilizing process that began with Coney Island amusements.

By the early 1990s the theme park form had almost fully developed the civilizing apparatus. Members of the park's management team, as well as auditors who came in to improve worker performance, would sometimes discuss their efforts of bringing rule to the unruly masses of both customers and workers. Theoretically, by costuming workers, scripting their interactions with patrons and teaching them codes of social interaction, management could change the worker. The same process was applied to the patron, who also, in the mind of management, needed to be tamed. By using the whimsical associations of the Looney Tunes characters and merchandizing, by immersing people in the fantastical theme lands of the park and by distracting them with thrilling rides, the everyday person could become, like Olmsted's masses, more civilized.[16] Though patrons commonly became upset with service at the park, and would often take this out on workers, they never complained about the loveable cartoon characters and Looney Tunes merchandise that dotted the park.

The taming effects of the theme park began with Walt Disney's efforts to clean up the amusement park. Even though the parks of Coney Island managed people's amusements, Walt Disney believed that more was needed. What was required was a killing of the carnival that lurked in the heart of every amusement park – and a symbolic and existential relocation of it. To clean up the amusement park, Walt Disney calculated the need for complete control of the operation. A key moment occurred when Disney conquered not the theme park but the land itself. Using secret real estate deals in Orlando, Florida, Disney quickly gobbled up the landscape, allowing for Walt Disney World to be opened many years after Walt Disney's death.[17] In the process Disney achieved the rare status of a private corporation receiving public governance rights. Through its pressure on the Florida legislature Disney sets its own taxes, has its own utilities company (Reedy Creek Improvement District) and is given almost complete control of the land. Had Disney wanted it, it could even have built its own nuclear reactor on its grounds.[18] Walt suggested that his style of community renewal could not be accomplished in a preexisting area; what he wanted was 'starting from scratch on virgin land'.[19] By having control of the land and all necessary resources like utilities and public works, Disney ensured that it could manage the entirety of the theme park. The effect is revolutionary and one that is often unnoticed when theme parks are disregarded as merely places of amusement. One of Walt Disney's designers once said that Disney is 'counter-life . . . I think we need something to counteract what modern society – cities –

Viewed from above, Disneyland displays its revolutionary model in total.

have done to us'.[20] Like Walt Disney's statement in the epigraph of this chapter, a theme park was not a fantasy – the outside world is the fantasy. Or as Jean Baudrillard said, 'Disneyland is presented as imaginary in order to make us believe that the rest is real.'[21]

One of the greatest developments of the theme park is the adoption of the themed ride. The early parks of Coney Island, particularly Luna and Dreamland, used thematic associations like the moon, hell and numerous fantastical places like Pompeii to create a fantasy setting. However, thematic development was often minimal and until theme parks achieved the capital necessary in the 1950s there was no concerted effort to develop themed rides that would create memorable connections with patrons on a par with movies. A popular film like *Star Wars* not only impacts the viewer through her appreciation of the film, but her reception of it makes her more open to future elaborations of the film as a brand. *Star Wars* collectibles like action figures are not popular because they are action figures but because they are associated with the strong memory people have of the *Star Wars* films. Likewise, the major themed ride can create associations between itself and the patron that will last a lifetime.

Disneyland's Pirates of the Caribbean is a themed ride that has proved the branding power not just of the theme park but of individual elements within it. The famous Disney dark ride involves visitors taking an indoor boat journey in search of Captain Jack Sparrow, and along the way encountering pirate battles, blazing towns and supernatural elements like skeletal pirates. Like many of Walt Disney's theme park attractions, Pirates utilizes audio-animatronic technology and enhances patrons' experiences by involving them in the middle of the major action of the loose narrative. On numerous Internet fan pages dedicated to the ride people state that they love the ride for its enduring themes, its sense of adventure and for making them feel like they are right in the middle of the action. Rides like Pirates of the Caribbean often create intergenerational effects in which parents pass down to their children the idea of the ride and, most importantly, their reminiscences of it from their past. Though the ride will become a brand, it appears more innocently as a material embodiment of a fantasy story and thus people 'pass it along' as if it were a part of their own intimate family history. One theme park watcher or Disney enthusiast, who frequents Disney parks on a weekly basis, when asked about his seeming obsession offered that 'I've been doing it so long, it defines me', but when pressed about why he likes theme parks so much, he could only say 'It would be nice to know why I love them.'[22] I have spoken to many people who, like this individual, are ultimately unable to say why they love theme parks, just that they do.

Pirates of the Caribbean exemplifies an important principle of the theme park as brand – namely, an attraction (or theme park) must be created in a way that will connect with people in an intimate sense, similar to Kevin Roberts' concept of the 'lovemark'.[23] He suggests that successful brands will be lovemarks, or 'the charismatic brands that people love and fiercely protect'.[24] On the Internet fans of Pirates of the Caribbean express their concerns about changes to the ride and display a sense of loyalty that parallels that of sports fans with their teams. Rides like Pirates exemplify the lovemark's characteristics of mystery (as something revealed through a compelling story or a dream), sensuality (the senses are used to make people connect with the concept) and intimacy (people become attached to the brand through commitment, empathy and passion).[25] Pirates of the Caribbean also ushered in a new trend that would continue with the Haunted Mansion: the transformation

of the theme park ride into a movie, further branding an already branded commodity and creating even greater intertextuality between theme parks and the cinema.[26]

As themed rides develop as proper cultural icons, on a par with other film, novel and toy icons, they become legitimated as cultural purveyors. Corporations soon discover that their multi-sensory, immersive and reflexive approaches to telling a story while also delivering a product make themed rides effective marketing tools. In some cases theme rides or major attractions, like the Las Vegas Hilton's Star Trek, The Experience, are built in order to draw on pre-made audiences. While many people would not venture to the off-Strip Hilton to experience the rides, museum and themed restaurant of the attraction, *Star Trek* fans would. So theme parks and themed spaces have begun to advertise to niche or boutique markets, reflecting the specialized demographics of the contemporary world. Simultaneously, theme parks offer patrons multiple

The Jaws ride at Universal Orlando illustrates the powerful synergy of movies and theme park rides.

takes on popular culture. At venues like Universal Studios, Jaws and other simulation rides allow patrons to 'ride the movies' and offer them an experience that involves them getting inside a commodity with which they are already familiar.

Shijingshan Amusement Park, in Beijing, China, uses the motto, 'Disneyland is too far, so please come to Shijingshan', and offers numerous features that are remarkably similar to those of Disney theme parks. Many costumed characters in the park look like the iconic ones made popular, and trademarked, by the Disney corporation: Snow White, the Seven Dwarves, Mickey Mouse, Goofy, Donald Duck and Shrek. The park also features a replica of Cinderella Castle and a ride that resembles Big Thunder Mountain Railroad. The park's owner, in response to a reporter's question about Shijingshan Amusement Park being a Disney copy on a Japanese television station, says that the characters and rides are, in fact, not copies. In terms of 'Mickey Mouse', he says that it is really a cat with big ears, while 'Cinderella' is a 'Chinese country

Quark's Bar and Restaurant, a contemporary form of theming inside a restaurant.

girl'. Later, a park employee working at a game stand that offers Disney-looking stuffed animals proclaims, 'This is Mickey!'[27]

A second such park, Nara Dreamland near Nara, Japan, closed in 2006. Like Shijingshan the theme park had features very similar to those of Disney theme parks, notably the iconic (but degraded) castle, a Matterhorn mountain, a main street section, a ride similar to the Jungle Cruise (called 'Adventure Jungle Cruise'), a 'Tomorrowland' section and a monorail and park train.[28] Both theme parks suggest an interesting reality of the contemporary theme park. As amusement parks are cleaned up and as they are infected with the technologies of theming, they reflect an understanding that in order to compete in the contemporary branded world, distinctive brands must be developed or, in some cases, copied. Brands have evolved into distinctive stories that reflect our most powerful and most intimate ideas, even if we do not recognize such stories as being connected to consumerism.

The defunct Japanese theme park, Nara Dreamland, with its suspiciously similar, yet degraded, copy of Disney.

The amusement parks of Coney Island spawned their own 'copies', parks that sprang up all over the country. However, such copies were often examples of using the original park's name only – such as Luna Park – not necessarily reproducing attractions, rides or architectural details from the original. There was, however, a practice of exporting similar rides from one park to the next, especially monumental recreations like the Battle of the Monitor and the Merrimac, which opened at Elitch Gardens in Denver, Colorado, shortly after it closed in 1910 at Luna Park. Many post-Coney Island amusement parks expanded as a result of new forms of technology, including the trolley car in the United States. By the 1920s as many as 2,000 amusement parks dotted the American landscape, but that number fell to 368 by 1948, in part due to changing economic conditions and the rise in popularity of the automobile.[29] Not until the corporate model of Disneyland, and later Six Flags, would the theme park be revived as a major form of public amusement, and it is no surprise that it is the brand that saves it. As the theme park has evolved into the twenty-first century, some parks have copied the Disney formula – some to extremes like Shijingshan Amusement Park and Nara Dreamland – but others have deliberately avoided the Disney and Six Flags models. Eschewing corporatism, branding and sanitized entertainment, parks like Blackpool Pleasure Beach, Kennywood and Knoebels instead present amusement for amusement's sake, akin to George Tilyou's original formula. The tension between the regional amusement park and the corporate Disney style theme park remains, and it is as telling as the debates between fast food and slow food, between GMOs and locally grown food and between globalization and anti-globalization.

Harry Potter is synonymous with the power of the brand. As a 4 billion dollar industry, Harry Potter is one the most successful

synergistic branding efforts of the twenty-first century. The Potter phenomenon began with the novels of J. K. Rowling, and spawned into motion pictures, numerous toys and educational products, and even a theme park. The Wizarding World of Harry Potter, part of the Universal Orlando Resort, will open in 2009. Due in large part to the popularity of the Potter brand, this new literary theme park – interestingly billed as a 'theme park within a theme park' – will seek to connect with the legions of fans who have already been introduced to Potter through the books, films and merchandise.[30] While theme parks may inspire trends within popular culture – as Disneyland did in many respects – The Wizarding World of Harry Potter illustrates that theme parks, as significant delivery vehicles or carriers of popular culture, are apt venues in which to situate the already popular brands and narratives of popular culture.

Even Hogwarts castle is recreated at The Wizarding World of Harry Potter at Universal Orlando.

One of the reasons that Potter fits in nicely with the theme park is the fact that both rely on narrative. As one branding expert suggested, 'Storytelling is the management method of the moment. "Tell the tale, make the sale" is the order of our day.'[31] The press releases for the Universal Potter theme park emphasize the story as the basis for the theme park. Stories derive their power in part due to their ability to convey a truth without appearing to do so. In the case of Potter the brand was established as a result of the universal appeal of Harry Potter – the books were translated into over 60 languages (thus breaking cultural barriers worldwide), the films helped connect to the powerful visual instincts of people (thus expanding the brand into multiple sensory channels) and the brand image of Potter resulted in people purchasing owls as pets and increases in applications to boarding schools (thus making

The popularity of J. K. Rowling's novels is elaborated in a cross-media sense at Universal Orlando.

Potter 'real' outside of its narrative confines). When the Potter brand becomes a theme park people will 'experience the world of Harry Potter in person', which is ironic given the fact that the theme park will re-imagine the already imagined worlds of J. K. Rowling.[32] This irony helps illustrate the unique meeting of the brand and the theme park.

The desire to inhabit the world of Hogwarts and Potter magic suggests an important truth of the theme park as brand. As popular culture evolves, the theme park develops more intimate and intertwined connections with it. Because theme parks are such successful purveyors of popular culture, and because they do not simply imagine fantasy but materialize it, they are used to pick up the hottest ideas, consumer trends or brands and give them a place. In an Anheuser Busch annual report the SeaWorld theme park was described as a 'positive setting to showcase our products'.[33] In the case of SeaWorld, like any theme park, multiple merchandizing of products is emphasized, but unique to this park is its use of the popular killer whale as an icon. One market research study conducted by the company found that 70 per cent of the profits coming in were due to the presence and visibility of killer whales.[34] The whale literally becomes a brand that is used by the theme park both to separate itself from competitors and to connect patrons with the powerful and profitable icon of the animal. SeaWorld, like all contemporary theme parks, fulfills a role as a '"selling machine" . . . capable of marketing the theme park to an unprecedented degree'.[35]

In addition to using animals as brands, theme parks regularly use the celebrity lives of famous people to establish a distinctive experience as well as a meaningful narrative to theme a venue. Dollywood uses the recognizable image of Dolly Parton, and her associated life history, as a branded phenomenon. Throughout

Dollywood, Parton's life is connected to visions of authentic crafts, goods, performances and rides. While a person, even a celebrity like Parton, may seem like an unlikely choice for a brand, when combined with the spatial narrative of the theme park, Dollywood becomes a branded expression of the life and music of Dolly Parton.[36] What makes the brand more meaningful, as well as more innocent, is the association of the person with the real event. Many celebrities, including Parton, struggled early in life and only later succeeded. In a romantic and Promethean sense the person as brand establishes a connection with people who, due to their middle-class status, may also feel a sense of struggle in their lives. Plans are in the works for a Bruce Lee theme park near Hong Kong. Though Lee was born in the United States, the marketability of his image led to a proposed park that will feature a roller coaster that emits the characteristic grunts of the martial arts actor, a martial arts academy and historical tributes to the late actor.[37] Even non-theme park spaces, like airports, use the celebrity as a brand to increase recognition of their venues. Liverpool John Lennon Airport uses the biographical theming of John Lennon to increase the popularity of its space.[38]

Animals and people find powerful roles in the branded theme park, in part because they are natural forms through which to tell a story and in which to personalize the story and ultimately connect to the lifeworld of the patron. As is discovered in the spaces of lifestyle theming and third spaces, the power to connect the brand to the most intimate, inner core of the patron is the ultimate goal. But people and animals may not be the safest of marketing options for theme parks. While Dolly Parton is recognized by many, she does fit into a niche of country music. More saleable commodities – the cartoon, feature film and television show – provide the theme park with a broader branding appeal.

Walt Disney's animated creations such as Mickey Mouse and Donald Duck laid a foundation for the theming of rides and the use of live cartoon characters in the theme park. The familiarity of such characters, particularly to children, provided a rich foundation for material branding within the theme park. Universal Studios has parlayed the popularity of *The Simpsons* into planned attractions at many of its theme parks, while Knott's Berry Farm features the Peanuts cartoon characters. Six Flags theme parks have employed the Looney Tunes characters, including Bugs Bunny, to make connections with children and their parents. What is significant in Six Flags' usage of cartoon characters is how the brand is spread throughout the theme park. At the now closed AstroWorld a themed Bugs Bunny Land featured cartoon Looney

Outside the Incredible Hulk Roller Coaster children live out their consumerist and branded fantasies.

Tunes actors, children's rides and other renditions of the Looney Tunes theme. Throughout the park costumed characters interacted with children, and shops and concession stands offered patrons Looney Tunes memorabilia.

Numerous television shows and movies have also been transformed into theme park rides, stunt shows and other attractions. To the list of *Fear Factor, Wayne's World*, Nickelodeon, *The Twilight Zone, Monsters Inc.*, The Wiggles, *Men in Black, I Love Lucy, Twister, The Blues Brothers, Shrek, Jimmy Neutron, Revenge of the Mummy, Twister, Jaws, Backdraft*, Curious George, *Terminator, Aliens, Beetlejuice, SpongeBob SquarePants, Indiana Jones, Star Wars, Jurassic Park, E. T., Earthquake* and the Muppets could be added hundreds of additional media offerings that have been adapted into the theme park. Though rides or stunt shows, movies, animated films and television shows often share cinematic principles, the translation of a film into a ride is often a limited enterprise. Yet the commodity, which is often owned by the same parent company that owns the theme park, can be marketed across multiple channels of the theme park experience. Six Flags AstroWorld's Batman the Escape, for example, featured a ride that was themed in accord with characters and situations from the Batman films, while a gift shop, which patrons had to move through after the ride, featured hundreds of products related to the Batman property: shirts, mugs and glassware, games, toys and videos. All theme parks, even amusement parks that avoid corporatism and theming, emphasize the selling of goods and services that have a larger connection to the world outside the park, but the difference is that the contemporary theme park integrates brands across the park – from rides to shows to gift shops to restaurants – and further naturalizes the patron's roles in consuming the goods and services associated with the theme park.

One of the most interesting branding phenomena of the contemporary theme park is the theme park as a brand. A number of theme parks use the brand not simply as a means of increasing the familiarity of their attractions or even selling more products, they do so because it is their identity.

Legoland has theme parks in England, Germany, Denmark and the United States. The United States version, in Carlsbad, California, is divided into eight theme lands, including Dino Island, Explore Village and Miniland USA. Like other theme parks Legoland has theming that creates a consistent architectural and peformative elaboration of each land, but the main difference is that Legoland uses the commodity brand form – the popular Lego toy – as the conduit that connects all of the attractions to each theme land and each theme land to the park as a whole. In Explore Village patrons can experience Safari Trek which, like the famous Jungle Cruise of Disney, includes an experience in which children

At Legoland California patrons experience a journey down a reconstructed world made up of Lego.

can 'venture into the wilds of Africa'.[39] The difference is that at Legoland the animals are made of Lego. Like other theme parks, including Disney's Epcot, Legoland features replicas of the major structures of the world but the twist at this park is that these forms are also made of Lego. The theme park features one of every Lego product, or about 4,500 SKUs (Stocking Keeping Units) of merchandise.[40] Lego is one of the most endearing toys, and has made its way into culture beyond the toy. Artists like Nathan Sawaya have transformed Lego into museum pieces that typically fetch tens of thousands of dollars, and the popularity of Legoland illustrates that Lego, like many commodity forms, has an intimate connection with the consumer.

Hersheypark in Pennsylvania opened in 1907 to provide a leisure space for Hershey Chocolate Company employees. In the years since then it has become a very popular theme park, in large part due to its playing off of the popular chocolate and confectionery brand. Though the park's theme lands are not themed in accord with candy, many other features of the park are, including plush cartoon characters like Reese's Peanut Butter Cup and Hershey's Kiss, who walk around and interact with children in parades. Many of the park's restaurants, including upscale ones, offer chocolate desserts based on Hershey's candy. Throughout the world the brand is increasingly mobilized not simply as a brand but as a brand that is realized within space. In Abu Dhabi there are plans to build a Ferrari theme park based on the popular automobile brand.[41] Another major corporation, Hard Rock, which began in London, has opened a theme park in Myrtle Beach, South Carolina, that is based on its famous branding of rock and roll and food. The Hard Rock Hotel and Casino in Las Vegas is a combination of casino gaming, rock and roll theming and rock and roll memorabilia arranged in a manner typically reserved for museums.

In a press release for the theme park representatives state that the park will reflect 'the brand's commitment to music', emphasizing how theme parks that are completely themed around brands must justify their commodity allegiance through the idea that the brand is not a brand but a reflection of lifestyle, identity and human values.[42] Many such branded parks and entertainment spaces use the argument that a holistic, branded venue will allow 'for a fuller experience of the brand', again de-emphasizing the idea that what people are mainly experiencing is a commodity form.[43] The brand as mobilized in architecture, performance and shopping experiences conveys the idea of the corporate form as *the* symbolic connector that links people, ideas and things in the theme park and, ultimately, as the entity that gives meaning to people and their experiences.

Theme parks have achieved the status of brands, but they are much more than this. They are material delivery spaces in which the ideas of consumer society are instilled in people. The universal features of theme park brands – the Pirates of the Caribbean ride, Disneyland's Cinderella Castle, Universal's Jaws ride and others – are translatable beyond the countries in which they originated. Of course brand images, even when created in the hospitable spaces of theme parks, are not universal. Like all products of the mind, they are conditioned by culture and are thus products of the culture. When theme parks are translated they must produce the branded space in a way that is acceptable to the patrons of the new culture. Many such theme park translations have been met with significant controversy.

In 1992 Euro Disneyland, later called Disneyland Resort Paris, opened in Paris, France. The park's opening was met with protests, negative journalism and scathing criticism from French intellectuals, politicians and citizens. A French journalist described the park

on its opening as 'a horror made of cardboard, plastic and appalling colors, a construction of hardened chewing gum and idiotic folklore taken straight out of comic books written for obese Americans'.[44] Studies of Euro Disneyland pointed to the fact that the adaptation of this new Disney theme park failed to grasp the local cultural contexts necessary to create a park pleasurable to the masses.[45] Many French citizens viewed certain prescriptions of the park, including stringent dress and grooming codes, as anti-French. Other concerns were raised about the lack of alcohol at the park, and soon, so as to better conform to French culture, the park served alcohol at its restaurants. Subsequent studies of the adaptations of Disney theme parks to non-western nations, however, have shown that contrary to notions of American cultural imperialism, Disney theme parks may actually be examples of the 'active

The theme park presents numerous icons that stick in all of our minds.

appropriation of Disney'.[46] As more theme parks that reflect an American origin are adapted to non-American cultures, further attention will be given to connecting the theme park to the traditions of the local culture. Of course, because the primary form being adapted is non-native, this is easier said than done.

The case of Euro Disneyland makes explicit the fact that as branded forms theme parks necessitate social debate over the nature of public amusements. Far from being flippant or surface forms of public amusement, theme parks are revealed as places of depth. As branding continues to be deployed in theme parks – especially in the model of an entire theme park (Disney) as a brand that can be plopped down in another culture – social controversies as tense and as involved as those that occur outside theme parks will heighten.

Moving and peformative experiences like the Mirage's volcano bring to life Walt Disney's 'weenie'.

Walt Disney often spoke of architecture and technology as functioning in the form of a 'weenie' – as something that would beckon the customer to go inside a space or cause the customer to go in a particular direction in a theme park. The weenie acts as a 'reward. If you have a corridor, at the end there has to be something to justify you going that distance.'[47] One of the primary ways in which non-theme parks spaces have adopted the theme park form is through a dramatic header such as a sign or event that attracts consumers to the space. In Las Vegas the dramatic volcano of the Mirage performs every hour, to the delight of tourists. The multisensory experience of the volcano attracts people, giving a sense of place to a consumerist spectacle. The erupting architecture of the Mirage, like the iconic buildings of the 1915 Panama-Pacific Exposition, provides an identifying mark that communicates the distinctiveness or brand of the casino. The volcano becomes synonymous with the theme which is, in turn, synonymous with the Mirage brand.

As the Mirage takes from the theme park, the weenie is the brand mobilized in space. More and more, the weenie – though much less garish and more disguised than the Mirage's volcano – has extended the theme park into the emerging world of lifestyle theming. As the store becomes a 'theme park' the technologies common to the theme park – most notably theming, but also interactive technology, spectacular architecture, the promotion of immersive and reflexive consumer experiences and the use of narrative or storytelling techniques – are incorporated within this new space. In many cases brands, rather than actual products themselves, are the outcomes of these new 'theme parks'.[48] As Paul Goldberger writes, 'the merchandise is secondary to the experience of being in this store, an experience that bears more than a passing resemblance to a visit to a theme park'.[49]

The lifestyle store is a response to the growing obsolescence of the traditional shopping mall and it uses the powerful approaches of the theme park to better conceal and further expand its brand. Lifestyle and flagship venues are found throughout the world. The most common forms include restaurants (ESPN Zone, Dave & Buster's, NASCAR Cafe, Rainforest Cafe) and retail stores (Niketown, REI Flagship Store, NBC Experience Store, Discovery Channel Flagship stores, M&M World, Whole Foods). They have in common the use of theme park techniques, including the architectural weenie, the creation of a 'place' of consumption, the exploration of a narrative or story and the expression of an inward-directed experience that directly involves the patron to

At Niketown in London's Oxford Street, lifestyle is brought full-circle: the theme park feels as if you are at home.

express an intimate connection of the brand and the consumer. What is unique about the new lifestyle, boutique or flagship store is the expression of a specific facet of the lifeworld of the consumer. Whereas a theme park typically covers all aspects of life, the lifestyle venue emphasizes one or a few aspects. Spaces like ESPN Zone, owned by Disney, focus on the powerful lifestyle associations between people and sports. At ESPN Zone patrons can enjoy American bar food, watch sporting events on gigantic television sets and partake in many video games and virtual forms of entertainment.

Like ESPN Zone, the flagship store emphasizes a key facet of lifestyle, typically a market trend such as electronics, the outdoors or the idea of athletics. At the London Niketown there is a re-created town in which buildings reference different types of sports: basketball, tennis, running etc. In the middle of the town is a square where events are held, including celebrity athlete appearances, and where images of sports are projected to customers. Niketown is not simply a means of establishing the love of the Nike brand, it also helps 'establish Nike as the essence not just of athletic wear but also of our culture and way of life'.[50]

NikeTown illustrates how brands can create a sense of identity in a world increasingly characterized by isolation and doubt, and another series of new themed spaces seeks to do even more. In these 'total themed spaces' there is an attempt to re-create, in full, an environment or place. At the Phoenix Seagaia Resort in Miyazaki, Japan, one of the greatest efforts at a total themed space was Ocean Dome. Like the traditional theme park the Ocean Dome attempted to create a total space that did not just contrast with the outside world, it fully replaced it. At the time of its opening the Ocean Dome was the largest indoor water park in the world, holding up to 10,000 people in a climate-controlled structure that guaranteed perfect beach conditions any day of the year.[51] Lush palm trees highlighted the rocky wall features, sand dotted the synthetic shores, a giant mural offered the visual appeal of a blue sky with clouds, a retractable roof provided a perfectly blue sky even on rainy or cloudy days, while people lounged on the beach, others surfed and some swam with toys traditionally used at real beaches. Integrated into the synthetic beach world was a smoking and erupting volcano, Caribbean carnivals and performances at night, and other water-themed adventures like white-water rafting. Due to low attendance the Ocean Dome closed in 2007, but its closure is marked by similar 'total themed spaces' opening in other parts of the world. The Tropical Islands Dome, part of the Tropical Islands in Krausnick, Germany, topped Ocean Dome with

At Ocean Dome (now closed) the ideal of recreating nature inside a theme park was achieved to a frightening degree.

an even larger indoor tropical beach environment. An abandoned aeroplane hangar the size of eight football fields and tall enough to fit the Statue of Liberty inside (standing up) involves a tropical environment even more expansive than the one in Japan. Inside, various cultural places associated with water are recreated for the customer – an Inipi Sweat Lodge, an Angkor Wat Temple that claims to be 'just like the original in Cambodia', a Waiotapu Spring Pool, based on thermal reserve pools in New Zealand, and others. Like the traditional theme park, the Tropical Islands Dome uses referencing of other places to create popular amusement but, in line with the new world of branding, it refocuses the purview of the theme park on one major element – water and associated tropical paradise.[52]

After spending their time in the Dome, patrons can participate in indoor camping inside the rainforest: 'We offer a range of tents in different sizes. All tents are equipped with mattresses, sheets, blankets and pillows. For a real nighttime Tropical adventure!'[53] Whether people will accept their virtual beach experiences inside an abandoned industrial hangar as meaningful and 'real' is debatable. Just as the psychological effects of the facades of Disneyland may promote people avoiding the brands, logos and predetermined narratives of theming – as in the phenomenon of experiencing Disneyland on acid or other controlled substances – the 'total themed spaces' of the Tropical Islands Dome may promote similar diversion from the intended meanings. On Internet file-sharing sites like Flickr, visitors to the Tropical Islands Dome show themselves in bathing suits, in front of murals and architectural features of Polynesian thatched huts and the oceans and sipping Piña Coladas, but what is fascinating about such travel journals is their emphasis on the fakeness of their 'tropical' exploits. While more theme parks and themed spaces will emerge, depending on their material and cultural approaches they may indeed invite a more ironic and critical form of tourism.

The theme park often reflects life but is a more exaggerated version of it. The lifestyle and flagship venue, in contrast, magnifies one aspect of life (such as sports) and expands on it through thematic means. Performance, themed architecture, service-focused customer service, entertainment and a sense of fantasy are all combined to produce effects similar to those found within the theme parks of Disney, Six Flags and Universal Studios. As these theme park elements are combined the consumer is brought closer to brands and, in the process, the customer's lifeworld is overlapped with the branded world of the company. The spirit of the culture merges with the brand and just as the theme park begins to lose its identity in a world that increasingly looks like a theme park, the branded world of the lifestyle and flagship store becomes indistinguishable from the world of the consumer.

One of the challenges of understanding the theme park as a branded form is locating the traditional aspects of the theme park – such as Coney Island's penchant for varied amusements, social upheaval and previously unknown kinetic, visual and other sensory experiences – within the corporate vision of the world. As Sharon Zukin expressed of Disney theme parks, 'Disney's success indicates a way to build economic development from an entirely cultural – that is, a "nonproductive" – base.'[54] While early amusement parks could be viewed as unproductive in terms of their creation of fantasy and themed spaces, they were productive in that they provided important social functions for people who visited them. The question for today's branded theme park and themed space is whether these new spaces fulfil similar functions. In China one of the most unique adaptations of the theme park as brand is the megamall.

South China Mall in Dongguan – a 9.58 million square foot (90,000m^2) monstrosity of shopping, with 1,500 stores, nearly three times the number of stores at America's Mall of America – appears to redefine the traditional theme park. While described as a shopping mall, the site includes theme lands common to a theme park, all of which highlight water cities: San Francisco District with upscale shopping and lush trees; Rain Forests District with an IMAX and log flume rides; Caribbean Sea District with Asian food delicacies and gardens; Amsterdam District with Van Gogh's artwork and spas, windmills and tulips; California Beach District with features from California, including a reproduction of the Hollywood sign; Champs-Élysées District with a recreation of the Champs-Élysées and a full-sized reproduction of the Arc de Triomphe; and Venice District with Venetian canals and gondolas. According to the mall's website, 'shopping is no longer a nuisance, but an enjoyment of life'.[55] Like a traditional theme park South China mall uses the theme land to associate characteristics and moods with a place – enchanting with Amsterdam, elegant and romantic with the Champs-Élysées, mysterious and passionate with Venice and adventurous with rain forests – but in this case, the association is even more focused on the processes of consumption. Within traditional theme parks there are activities that focus on non-consumption, but the now struggling South China Mall seems to indicate a movement more in line with patterns of consumption. The mall's motto of shopping without nuisance illustrates the ways in which technologies of the theme park are increasingly deployed for purposes of lifestyle consumption.

As megamalls, flagship and lifestyle stores and themed restaurants expand worldwide, the image of the theme park will continue to be transformed. Even within the world of coffee

The interior of the New York-New York, Las Vegas, with smoking manhole covers, illustrates the concept of microtheming.

shops, the influence of the theme park is felt. The spaces of quasi-theme parks, like those of the New York–New York Hotel and Casino in Las Vegas, feature spaces that not only promote brands but make them comforting – something which the mega-mall may have difficulty achieving due to its scale and overwhelming features. Microtheming, in which a space uses theme park architecture and perspective, provides the customer with a sense of place. Even small details, like fire hydrants and smoking manhole covers, are recreated in the small village of the New York–New York's take on New York City.[56] Theming is now commonly used to create a sense of place and a comfort with the brand in franchises like Starbucks. Starbucks uses the idea of the 'third place' – meaning a social site for people that is in between the home and the workplace – to create hominess, authenticity, brand distinction and patron connection.[57] Such new third places are quickly becoming the cultural equivalents of the pub and cafe traditions in the United Kingdom and Europe.

Third places like Starbucks illustrate an interesting and ironic twist for the theme park as brand. While traditional ideas of the brand emphasized the distinctiveness of what was being marked, the newest form of the brand, as it travels from the amusement park to the theme park and then to the quasi-theme park and the themed space, is now losing its sense of distinction. As more venues attempt to replicate the distinctiveness of theming found in successful third spaces a new form of the theme park is born. It is a form that looks nothing like the fantasy spaces of Luna Park and Dreamland, nor even like the sanitized spaces of Disneyland; instead, it looks like our favourite local cafe.

Many studies of the theme park take aim at the ways in which the theme park promotes escapism and creates simulated and homogeneous representations, and other studies have emphasized

not simply their representational effects but their transformative ones. As one theorist expressed of Disneyland, 'The contrast between conditions inside the theme park, where everything seemed to work, and conditions outside, where nothing seemed to work, led many to conclude that the world ought to model itself as closely as possible after Disneyland.'[58] What happens with the theme park revolution is much more than the introduction of a new way of entertaining the masses. As the architectural, performative and cultural aspects of the theme park spread, the theme park gains a greater grip on the world while simultaneously losing

The distinctive 'third place' ambiance of Starbucks: aroma, decor, comfort in one space.

its form. The most profound evolution of the branded theme park occurs when the theme park becomes invisible, when it affects people without leaving noticeable traces of its operations.

The theme park nation, as James Howard Kunstler suggested when describing the rapid forms of social and urban growth in the areas near or inspired by theme parks – 'a land full of places that are not worth caring about will soon be a nation and a way of life that is not worth defending' – has become a reality not just in the United States but in many nations across the world.[59] One critical study of Disney's effect on the outlying areas of Orlando, Florida, described the theme park nation as a process of architectural encroachment and a resultant uneasy new public culture:

> growth built on consumption, not production; a society founded not on natural resources, but upon the dissipation of capital accumulated else-where; a place of infinite possibilities, somehow held together . . . by a shared recognition of highway signs, brand names, TV shows, and per-sonalities, rather than any shared history. Nowhere else is the juxtaposition of what America actually is and the conventional idea of what America should be more vivid and revealing . . . Orlando is syn-onymous with the theme-park culture that has overtaken America.[60]

Yet this new era of the theme park nation is not just about brands, familiar architectural forms and shared consumer consciousness, it is much deeper.

Naomi Klein has said that 'Disney's branding breakthrough is a celebration of brandlessness, of the very public spaces the compa-ny has always been so adept at getting its brands on in the rest of its endeavors.'[61] What Klein pointed to was the movement of Disney's branding beyond the brand and into life itself. Like the theme park, when the brand is naturalized it loses connection to the company and becomes a natural part of the life of the consumer. The most profound expression of brandlessness is the community of Celebration, Florida. Celebration is a planned community of over 2,000 residents, complete with a school, shops and its own newspaper, *Celebration Independent*. Ironically, at Celebration, there are no explicit brands present. Unlike many communities in the United States, Celebration has no fast food, no franchising, no box stores. Celebration has no street named 'main', and thus distances itself from any associations with the many Disney theme parks in Orlando.[62] Like the lifestyle store and the themed restaurant, the planned community of Celebration is not a theme park, but in many ways it reflects the theme park as brand. The greatest product produced by Celebration is not a thrill ride, a dramatic recreation or a stunt show, it is people themselves, who are 'simultaneously, promoters of commodities and the commodities they promote'.[63]

Notably, the corporate form, as it is integrated with the theme park, creates a shift in the social dynamics of the theme park. Whereas early Coney Island amusement parks expressed a sociality of the masses – in which people came together in new and disruptive ways – the contemporary theme park, especially the Disney version, expresses an emphasis on the family and the individual within it as the primary social form. In striking contrast to the throwing together of people in George Tilyou's Pavilion of Fun, contemporary Disney theme park rides, like the popular Haunted Mansion, position families or groups of friends within enclosed capsule chairs. The effect makes it difficult to see people in the adjoining vehicles, except on some turns. Metaphorically, the cars represent the movement of theme park sociality into the domain of the family, which consumes on its own and experiences on its own, much like Margaret Thatcher's pronouncement that 'there is no such thing as society. There are individual men and women, and there are families.'[64] The theme park as brand impacts both the individual and the family as it charts a new direction for consumption and life itself. As it becomes a brand, its evolution is nearly complete. Now the only thing remaining is its apotheosis as an image of the mind, a text.

6 Theme Park as Text

No sooner does an object lose its concrete practical aspect than it is transferred to the realm of mental practices. In short, behind every real object there is a dream object.
Jean Baudrillard[1]

In 2006 a restaurant opening in Mumbai, India, attracted international outrage. Like many contemporary restaurants, this one featured themed decor, an involved menu and prominent signage but, unlike all others, this one focused on Adolf Hitler. According to restaurateur Puneet Sabhlok, 'Hitler is a catchy name. Everyone knows Hitler'.[2] Hitler's Cross signalled a new, disturbing trend of popular culture, and one that is rooted in the tradition of the theme park. The theme park began in the amusement traditions of Coney Island, with themed amusement spaces, rides and attractions that emphasized the enjoyment of the patron. As it evolved it focused more extensively on developing nuanced theme lands within its spaces, even using microtheming to provide incredibly detailed recreations of places. Then the brand provided the theme park with a more capitalist and consumerist focus, where the lives of people merge with the interests of the branded theme park. In its latest moment, the theme park achieves a mental image of itself, a text that like all texts can be variously read, interpreted, critiqued and remade. Jean Baudrillard has said that the object eventually loses its physicality and becomes a mental object and, in the case of the theme park, all that has come before has now been transferred into a text that can be deployed in arenas outside the theme park. Particularly as a form that affects people in

their lives, a theme park acts on non-material levels, impacting individuals in ways that Boyton, Tilyou, Thompson, Dundy and Reynolds could have never imagined.

In the case of Hitler's Cross an incredibly offensive idea was controversial in part due to poor taste and in part due to the textual status of the theme park. Especially in its branded form the theme park teaches business owners the powerful impact that its technologies, architectures and patterns can have. Theming, as a means of organizing a space in a unified and fantasy sense, has now become an architectural practice outside the theme park. Theming

In Mumbai, India, the controversial Hitler's Cross restaurant was forced to change its name and alter its decor due to its offensive theme.

is, in fact, a materialized and mobilized form of storytelling and as an overall form it becomes a text that is transferred from the world of theme parks to the world of themed spaces. Restaurants, hotels, museums, dental offices and even homes have become themed, declaring homage to the origins of the theme park form. The owner of Hitler's Cross said, 'I never wanted to promote Hitler . . . I just wanted to promote my restaurant.'[3] Of course, his explanation is inadequate, particularly as the associations of Hitler are anti-Semitism, genocide and totalitarianism. What is interesting about his explanation is his inability to see the offence behind the facade of his restaurant, as if all that matters is the theming itself and as if theming is somehow extra-political, extra-cultural. This helps illustrate the ways in which theming has expanded to include any and all spaces that people encounter in their daily lives. Eventually, the owners renamed the establishment Cross Cafe and, according to Sabhlok, 'no more dictators' will be featured in the theming of his restaurant.[4] Other themed spaces, including the Crash Cafe of New Jersey – which would have featured video screens of airplane crashes and a life-sized airplane crashing through the front of the place – the Civil War-themed Disney's America on the sacred grounds of Manassas, Virginia; the NRA SportsBlast in Times Square, New York City; and Dracula World in Romania were never built due to the controversy related to their themes.[5] What is paramount is not just that these spaces had controversial subject matters as their narratives, but that they were materialized – they were given a more vivid way to tell their controversial stories. Theming is the most profound example of the theme park as text. What theming allows is for any space to become like a theme park.

The controversial themed space like Hitler's Cross results in many people asking whether the theme park has gone too far. In the narrative worlds of author George Saunders the theme park has a most interesting apotheosis as a life form. In *Pastoralia* two 'Imagineers' work in a prehistoric theme park. For their guests they re-create what it was like to live in prehistoric times, making grunts, eating goats and avoiding any resemblance of their real-life selves in front of onlookers.[6] The performers attend to every detail of their re-creations, even when it seems contrary to who they are and even in the face of company pressures and forms of dehumanization. In *Civilwarland in Bad Decline* Saunders again takes the subject of the theme park, in this case a Civil War re-creation one, and offers a critique of its form as well as the society that finds value in it.[7] Gang problems in the park, the inability of workers to perform their scripted parts and concerns over the 'Verisimilitude Irregularities List' suggest a less than pristine status of the theme park. In Saunders's work the theme park takes on a humorous status in its new form as an

The theme park, as it emerges from the amusement park, threatens to leave the amusement park behind.

imaginative text. His many takes on it illustrate the popularity of this form of popular amusement as well as the criticisms that have been applied to it.

When the theme park becomes a literal text, as in the case of Saunders's work, it displays its new form. It moves from being a themed landscape full of thrill rides to a place of the mind – a mental image. As the theme park becomes appropriated in popular culture in various ways it begins to lose hold of its image. Though it increases in popularity as more and more places are themed, it also records a significant slippage: as the theme park becomes a text, its narrative is multiply modified, its authors are no longer the bosses and showmen of the past (Boyton, Tilyou, Thompson and Dundy and Reynolds) nor the storytellers of the near present (Disney, Wynne), but the theme park itself. Like the board game Monopoly or the photocopying technology known as Xerox, the theme park becomes actualized as a form that everyone knows, instantly. In its new status as a life form – as a text that can be recalled in nearly anyone's mind – the theme park takes on new authorship. The term 'theme park', like 'roller coaster', has become a common term of everyday life in numerous cultures. People call many things theme parks, even when they do not fit the bill – 'Vegas is an adult theme park', 'Iraq is a theme park for terrorists' and other variations. Though Iraq is not, of course, a theme park, it is envisioned in linguistic connection with a theme park. It becomes a 'conduit metaphor', reflecting a new status as a common, not fantastical, construction.[8] But what are the reactions to this new status of the theme park as a metaphor?

For some the slippage of the theme park from its once material state results in a desire to go back to how things once were. Fans of traditional amusement parks bemoan the loss of the theme

park to corporate giants like Disney and Six Flags, and many of them hold personal mental images of theme parks that contrast with the corporate image of the contemporary theme park. While once theme parks meant places of fantasy and enjoyment, the idea has now taken on sinister connotations. For some the theme park can be equated with anything that is about pure simulation, corporatism or clean, sanitized amusement. Alan Bryman has offered one such track in his thesis of the 'Disneyization of society'. According to him, Disneyization is 'the process by which the principles of the Disney theme parks are coming to dominate more and more sectors of American society as well as the rest of the world'.[9] Theming, hybrid consumption, merchandizing and performative labour are all, according to Bryman, incorporated in non-theme park venues in ways that challenge the authenticity and quality of these places.[10] The theme park, like other popular culture forms that have assented to a recognizable status, becomes a form that is so successful that it can be arguably applied to any space of everyday life. Critics like Bryman are concerned that this movement of the theme park form – as a cookie-cutter text that can plopped down on any space – will result in a loss of the authenticity of life. Like a virus, a terrorist or a moral panic, the theme park threatens everyday life itself.

The 1977 film *Rollercoaster*, in which a mad bomber uses popular amusements as weapons of mass destruction.

In the theme park's evolution as a text, an interesting moment occurs when the theme park is written as a site of disorder. In part this narrative is the result of criticisms of the theme park, offered by critics and everyday people, that express concerns about the ubiquity of theme parks in our lives. One of the first movies to focus on the theme park was the thriller *Rollercoaster* (1977). In the film a terrorist, played by Timothy Bottoms, devises a way to blackmail amusement park companies by placing radio-controlled bombs on amusement park roller coasters. In a tape-recorded message sent to the major park owners, the terrorist exclaims, 'Each of your companies is involved, either through wholly owned subsidiaries or long-term lease arrangement, with the amusement park industry. As you know, it's a peculiar business, more vulnerable than most. During the past week, I've given you two examples of just how vulnerable.' The plot centres on the fact that theme parks have become popular sites of public amusements and the idea that theme park companies will do anything to avoid the negative publicity associated with the terrorist's actions. The film, when premiered in theatres, featured Sensurround, a technology that consisted of large speakers that rocked the movie theatre during key scenes. In its adaptation of the roller coaster and the theme park to the register of film, *Rollercoaster* attempted to mimic their sensory conditions. It was the first of many films and books to play on the idea of the theme park as a site of danger. Though this seems ironic, play, especially the sort that is manifested in multi-million dollar theme park attractions, is deep, as the anthropologist Clifford Geertz suggested.[11] Deep play, of the sort portrayed in a theme park, reveals its interior, serious nature when the bomber in *Rollercoaster* transforms the roller coaster and the theme park from sites of pleasure into sites of death and destruction.

Many other narratives, including Robert Stuart Nathan's *Amusement Park*, Lincoln Child's *Utopia*, Michael Crichton's *Jurassic Park* and at least one film, *Thrill*, similarly ask us to meditate on the idea of the theme park as a site of potential disorder.[12] The tradition of the theme park, especially as reflected in classic novels that became movies – *Jurassic Park* and *Westworld* – expresses the moral missive of human experimentation with nature (genetics and dinosaurs in the first, humanlike robots in the second) and its ill effects. Thus the theme park as a narrative becomes a foundation on which the most serious issues of society – science, religion, morality and even the meaning of life – may be tested and played out. In *Westworld* (1973), written and directed by Michael Crichton, the theme park Delos is the home of three theme lands: Westworld, Medievalworld and Romanworld. For a high price wealthy tourists can come and enjoy surprisingly real theme lands that feature robots that allow the patrons to enact their fantasies. Unfortunately for the guests the park's realistic robots malfunction and begin killing the thrill seekers in the theme lands. The iconic Gunslinger, played by Yul Brynner, was programmed to always lose in gun duels with patrons but, following the meltdown in the theme park, the Gunslinger releases its own desires, throws aside the order of the park's simulated technologies and kills for real.

Westworld was followed by *Futureworld* (1976), in which the designers of the failed Delos park claim to have fixed the problems that had beset it. Using the new theme park the owners launch a scheme to take over the world by attracting the most influential world leaders to the park, taking genetic samples of them while they sleep and introducing cloned versions of them into the world. In *Futureworld* there is a noticeable shift from the idea of a theme park gone awry in its own controlled space to the technologies of the theme park and the motivations of its creators to move outside the theme park proper and take over the world. In *Westworld* the theme park is still confined to its own space, destined to collapse and take only those within its space with it, while in *Futureworld* it strives to take the entire world down with it. Though both films are science fiction narratives they offer insights about the tensions that the theme park faces in its apotheosis as a text. In the real world, in some people's minds, the narrative of the theme park gone awry and posing dangers to patrons and the theme of the ideas and technologies of the theme park infesting the world outside of its boundaries have already come true.

Popular amusements and especially theme parks have become more and more subject to moral considerations. Though the real dangers posed by ride catastrophes and workers with bad motives (the paedophiles in the concerns of Christian criticisms) are small, astronomically so, the motive behind such criticisms is much stronger. In texts like *Send a Message to Mickey* Southern Baptists and other denominations launch major attacks against everything Disney, including its theme parks: 'This is not Walt's Disneyland anymore . . . [in this] expose of Disney's dark side . . . You'll see why Christians opposing immorality in society is not optional but a vital part of communicating the mercy of God to a society in the process of decay.'[13] In this polemic biblical passages are interspersed with narrative details about the sinning going on in parks like Disneyland, all leading to a textual formation of the apocalypse taking place in, or perhaps being fuelled by, the likes of theme parks. Indeed, in the minds of many, Judgement Day will take place on a troika in a theme park. Because such criticisms have expanded within society, theme parks must respond to them and counter with their own public relations narratives.

For some, not only are their waking hours preferably spent at a theme park, but they wish to inhabit one after their passing. A recent phenomenon in some US theme parks is the scattering of a loved one's ashes on the park premises. Disneyland rides like Pirates of the Caribbean and the Haunted Mansion are two of the most common places where theme park patrons commit the remains of their loved ones to their final resting.[14] While it may surprise some that a person's life identity could be encapsulated in their final resting place at a theme park ride, this testifies to the profound roles that theme parks play in people's lives. No less surprising to some is the idea that the undead would haunt the simulated, consumer spaces of the theme park. On Internet discussion pages, theme park fans meditate on what might seem to be some of the strangest examples of the sacred. For some there are questions concerning park accidents that result in deaths, perhaps leading to the haunting of the rides with unhappy spirits. In other discussions, for instance of the popular Cedar Point park in Sandusky, Ohio, patrons speculate about phantom riders who apparently get upset if their favourite carousel horses are ridden by the living, or undead guests who have never checked out of the park's historic Hotel Breakers. In other tales, reminiscent of the plot of *The Five People You Meet in Heaven*, more benevolent ghosts protect theme park patrons by assuring that ride accidents will not occur, in some cases shutting down dangerous rides with their magical powers, in others helping to repair them. Some of the most benevolent of such spirits are the ghosts who are rumoured to assist in menial tasks, such as emptying trash from park trashcans.[15]

Perhaps even more uncanny are the ghosts that are said to haunt the paranormal and fantasy themed spaces of parks like Disney as if, like the humans whose remains are committed to their rides, these undead cannot get enough of the theme parks in life. At Walt Disney World's Pirates of the Caribbean, the spirit of a worker who died at the park is greeted by employees upon opening the ride, while at Epcot's Spaceship Earth a small girl with flowing blonde hair continually rides one of the attraction's cars and at the Tower of Terror the ghost of a small boy appears and disappears, confusing people as to whether apparitions on the ghostly ride are real ghosts or simulated, technological ones. It is perhaps not surprising that ghosts choose to inhabit theme parks since they play such meaningful roles in the lives of the living.[16]

The theme park as a sacred site – whether used by the living as the last places to remember their fallen loved ones or by the dead as afterlife theme parks – attests to the ways in which it has expanded beyond the original model. But as the theme park continues to move, as it expands as a text and interpretive object, numerous consequences emerge. In some cases theme parks are owned by large parent companies that have holdings in media, journalism and forms of popular culture outside the theme park industry. Disney has numerous holdings, including ABC television network, Pixar Animation Studios, Touchstone Pictures, Hollywood Pictures and Miramax Films. The company's broad assets allow for synergistic opportunities, including links between the world of theme parks and the world of movies. Disney has the ability to leverage incredible cultural power to tell stories in more ways than other theme parks can.

An irony of the era in which Disney's theme park model has expanded is that it has become too commonplace. Though Disney can control the behaviour of workers in its parks, and though it can motivate the actions of customers who enter the predetermined spaces, it cannot affect the image of Disney parks that is reflected in numerous places like the Internet. While working at

AstroWorld I was accustomed to the attention given to the image problem of the theme park – what did customers think of AstroWorld, and how could we improve any negative perceptions about the theme park? As the theme park expands in the world, it gets caught up in rumours, public interpretations, falsehoods and reinterpretations in various media. Disney theme parks are under constant scrutiny, and when an accident occurs it makes the news; deaths in Disney parks achieve an even more elevated status. As part of the larger textual genre of fantasy that characterizes mass consumer culture, theme parks are subject to the popular culture trend of rewriting. As a sort of Pandora's Box of consumerism, the theme park as a textual and discursive object becomes subject to multiple rewritings, reappropriations and revisionings.

Theme park workers are trained to avoid speaking with media representatives or offering them any information, and this is for good reason. Perceptions about the park's image can directly impact marketing efforts and can affect park attendance. For years critics have accused Disney theme parks of hiding information about crimes and of impeding investigations of the rare deaths that do occur on Disney property.[17] For some the image of

Films like *Final Destination 3* use the theme park as a reversal of its typical order – from pleasure to pain.

the theme park is a tarnished one. In their minds, Disneyland and associated theme parks – generally Six Flags, Universal and other Disney theme parks – have begun to exhibit undesirable characteristics. In the past, they believe, Disney-like theme parks promoted harmony, family-centred amusement, wholesomeness and clean entertainment, while in the present they argue that theme parks like those of Disney have become the opposite of their mental wish image: dirty, dangerous, erotic and characterized by debauchery. Stories of spying wardrobe attendants at Cinderella Castle masturbating, peeping on employees and even videotaping them create an image of Disney that contrasts with the clean one that it strives to maintain.[18] In another case Disneyland Paris cartoon characters were videotaped committing lascivious acts backstage while in their character costumes – Minnie Mouse is mounted by Goofy and an unidentified snowman character, while the chipmunks (Chip 'n' Dale) watch in delight. Later Mickey Mouse does the same to the snowman. Much to the chagrin of Disney, the tape, known as 'Mouse Orgy', appeared on many popular Internet video sites.[19] For theme park public relations officials the emphasis on managing and protecting the image of the theme park leads to an interesting textual obsession. As academics, journalists and laypersons fashion various interpretations of given theme park and their constituent parts, public relations officials attempt to limit the resultant text, especially if it has negative undertones.

While Disney and other major theme park corporations work diligently to control their image, to assure that their 'text' of the theme park does not become tarnished, in the new rhizomatic era of popular culture this is often impossible. Former Disney President Michael Eisner said, 'I would prefer ABC not to cover Disney. I think it's inappropriate.'[20] At the time ABC News was preparing a story on paedophiles working at Disney theme parks, but ABC executives stopped the story, fearing that it would tarnish the Disney image. In a similar attempt to control its theme park public relations, an Anheuser-Busch employee purportedly altered edits critical of SeaWorld on the popular Internet encyclopedia Wikipedia. Using a programme created by a computer scientist, the erasure of the phrase 'lack of respect toward its orcas' was traced to the corporate offices of Anheuser-Busch, the parent company of SeaWorld.[21] Much to the delight of corporations like Disney and Anheuser-Busch, their theme parks have expanded not just into public space but into mental space, but this expansion has surprisingly unintended and potentially democratic consequences. It is no longer the case that theme parks are the products of corporate executives or Imagineers, they are the products of everyday people who remake them using their own, albeit limited, logics and lifestyles.

The theme park, as suggested by the copies made of successful ones like those of Disney and Six Flags, becomes the victim of the virus that it created and from which it believed it had inoculated itself. Like bricolage, which involves a person remaking something old into something new, using the detritus of the world that has been left behind, the theme park as text is an emergent, hybrid and minority form.[22] For some this remaking of the theme park can occur inside it. Travelling with AstroWorld employees in the 1990s to other Six Flags parks I was introduced to 'theme park watchers', individuals whose passion for the 'right' theme park was manifested in a near-obsessive desire to fix things at a theme park.[23] On their trips to theme parks these fans could not contain their desire to pick up trash in the park, even though they were on vacation. For other fans, whether park workers or not, the desire to remake the theme park happens on the Internet. These watchers use the global communicative power of the Internet to get their words across to others. Whether detailing the failings of corporate decisions in a theme park, the tragedy of a new ride that lacks lustre or poor decisions to rework popular attractions, these individuals use the theme park as text – as something that they know intimately and will protect to the death – to offer their own authorship of something that has been, up to this point, an entirely corporate-driven story.

Another option is to make one's own theme park, and this form of the text has many permutations. It is unlikely that a person could afford to build her own theme park – Michael Jackson and his infamous Neverland Valley Ranch apart – so that creation may be limited. One possibility is creating a personalized theme park ride. Stories abound of coaster enthusiasts who cannot get enough of them, and in some cases build their own mock roller coasters – some out of toothpicks, others actually working models that function with the physics of the real theme park rides. In 2008, on the popular YouTube online video sharing website, at least 50 videos existed of backyard roller coasters. Such cases suggest that the theme park as text is a form of reverse engineering in which fans attempt to create their own version of an iconic theme park ride.[24] What such examples illustrate is that there is a special potential to the theme park ride. It is not simply ridden, but it is attached to the mind; the result is a unique transformation of the theme park as a material construct to a mental or textual one. Though the reverse engineered ride is ridden like the traditional theme park ride, the key is not its material fact but its imaginative one: it is given life, in a monstrous sense, by the everyday person.

Not surprisingly, video games have been an apt site in which to explore the remade theme park. In the 1990s simulation games became a popular choice of gamers and non-gamers worldwide who wanted to exert control in the face of the uncertainty of the real world. Like the scenarios depicted in the many novel and film portrayals of theme parks these computer versions suggest an image of an unstable and mutating theme park that the player/designer must tame.

A variety of theme park games has given players the opportunity to imagine the world of the theme park inside the comfort of their homes: *Theme Park Inc*, *Theme Park World*, *RollerCoaster Tycoon* (and its many sequels) and *Thrillville*. In these games players get to control the world of the theme park, including the planning of rides, the layout of the theme park, the theme of the park and its theme lands, the operational functions of the park (including maintenance, ride operations and entertaining patrons) and interacting with patrons in the park. In most of these games the theme park is on the verge of disorder, and the player must restore order by attending to rides, including dispatching maintenance men to them when they malfunction. The player must also build new concessions, shows and rides in order to meet the fickle wishes of the patrons. In some cases patrons express their lack of interest in a ride, while in others they show their delight. In *RollerCoaster Tycoon* importance is placed on the design of roller coasters, and some players post their own rides and theme parks that others may download on the Internet. In *Thrillville* the emphasis includes focusing on the desires of the patron, with whom the player may interact. While many of the theme lands and theme parks of these games often have an unreal feel to them – such as parks that are entirely themed around pirates – some attempts have been made to replicate the real theme parks of the world, including an expansion set for *RollerCoaster Tycoon* that features the rides of the popular Alton Towers park in the United

Kingdom. Games such as these represent the desire to simulate the worlds of everyday life, and they also represent the growth of the theme park as a primary form of public amusement. As people create their own theme parks and establish authorship of them they reflect on how the theme park has evolved into a global model and a text that is being constantly rewritten.

Disney's Virtual Magic Kingdom (closed in 2008) attempted to use cyberspace to simulate the theme parks that have made the company famous. In this virtual version of the theme park players controlled personalized avatars and moved through the familiar spaces of Main Street, Fantasyland and Adventureland. While inside the virtual theme park they could make friends, converse with one another, shop and complete quests inside the park with others. Like the real theme park, in the Virtual Magic Kingdom staff operated various attractions and helped players out in their navigation of

In Atari's video game *RollerCoaster Tycoon* the thrills of the theme park can be experienced in the comfort of one's home.

the online community. The virtual community Second Life, created by Linden Research Inc, is a popular virtual world that allows users to create their own original content. Unlike the structured Virtual Magic Kingdom, in Second Life users can fashion their own theme parks and invite others to enjoy them. The residents use themes in a way to represent their interests, including their fascination for certain forms of popular culture. In the virtual theme parks of Second Life visitors can ride roller coasters and enter the re-created lands of fairy tales and novels, including the *Wizard of Oz*, Prim Hearts and Neverland, a 48-acre theme park based on J. M. Barrie's *Peter Pan*. Though the theme park becomes a (public) text in these examples, it does remain a brand. Comcast, the cable and communications entertainment company, has created a space called Comcastic Island. The space includes car tracks, jetskis, jet packs and a concert and entertainment

Using the machinations of a home computer, anyone can create a theme park in a virtual sense, but is the ride experience as heart-pounding as it is in the 'real' theme park?

centre, all of which are themed around speed and thus highlight Comcast's business focus. Of course one question related to these virtual theme parks is whether the theme park will eventually lose its physical bearing in the world; will it become a purely virtual phenomenon?

The theme park, as it has moved away from the chaos that presumably characterized the early amusement parks (as well as associated spaces like carnivals and state fairs), has become associated with organization, sanitation and order. As such, it becomes the target of culture, particularly for those who find the theme park's emphasis on order to be a peculiar trait. As Bryman's argument

Theme parks allow people to experience existential, psychological and social states not possible in the real world.

suggested about the Disneyization of society, for some the theme park takes on a form that is loathed – it is, simply, going too far, a distortion and degradation of the real, authentic world. The popular animated show *The Simpsons,* which regularly pokes fun at all forms of popular culture, has frequently parodied the nature of theme parks. *The Simpsons'* versions of theme parks appear to be strikingly similar to real contemporary theme parks. In the episode 'I'm Goin' to Praiseland' close references to actual religious theme parks, such as the Holy Land Experience, are made, while in 'Hungry, Hungry Homer' an even more explicit focus is placed on contemporary branded theme parks like Legoland. In this episode Homer Simpson and his family visit Blockoland, a theme park based on a brand of interlocking block toys. Taking the idea of a branded theme park to an extreme, *The Simpsons* shows patrons entering Blockoland with a tram made of blocks (including square block wheels that produce a disquieting effect in the riders), children's slides with a block (bumpy) descent, a cruise ride in which the water is even made of blue blocks, and theme lands like Squaresville, Cube Country and Rectangle Land. The episode illustrates the bizarre side of theme parks, particularly the extent to which people will accept the crafted narratives of theme parks so intimately into their lives.[25] In a comedic way *The Simpsons'* take on the theme park revises the narrative of Plato's cave to include the simulated spaces of everyday life that, like the cave, are spaces of near addiction.

In the novel *England, England*, author Julian Barnes playfully addresses the proliferation of the theme park in the mind.[26] People crave the symbols of the English past and the present so much that the only solution to the longing and nostalgia that they feel – whether for the good life or for the loss of life in memory (as Marcel Proust would have it) – is to create landscapes that allow

for the good life to be maintained in materiality (the theme park) and played out in textuality (the mind of the visitor). In Barnes's novel the entrepreneur Sir Jack Pitman creates a theme park that is superior to both the theme park and the real England that England, England draws on for its simulations and recreations. Citizens of the world were polled to give Sir Jack a sense of what to reproduce at England, England and the respondents offered a list of 50 items that they considered to be the quintessence of England, including the Royal Family, Robin Hood, bowler hats, breakfast, BBC, Stonehenge, Marks & Spencer, bad underwear and the Battle of Britain. All in perfect, politically correct, clean and efficient form, there is a Harrods inside the Tower of London with

Something as simple as a theme park game projects itself in existential ways.

Beefeaters pushing patrons' shopping carts, Stonehenge, Anne Hathaway's Cottage, pre-stamped postcards, the White Cliffs of Dover, beetle-back taxis, a half-size Big Ben, the graves of Shakespeare and Princess Diana, Robin Hood and his Band of Merrie Men, and an authentic selection of puddings, crumpets and ales. According to a journalist's first-person report in the novel, 'The best of all that England was, and is, can be safely and conveniently experienced on this spectacular and well-equipped diamond of an Island.'[27] In this version of England, it is all 'more convenient, cleaner, friendlier, and more efficient . . . but not what traditionalists would call authentic'.[28] England, soon renamed 'Old England', eventually 'lost all sense of itself' and began to collapse under the weight of England, England's more powerful version.[29]

Memory, as a text of human experiences, offers the theme park one of the most significant forces that it redeploys to varying effect. In the fictional England, England the fears of Jean Baudrillard and Walter Benjamin – in which originals dwindle and are replaced by copies – are realized.[30] *England, England*'s play on memory suggests that the mental texts that we have of our favourite places and our history are somehow devalued by the theme park form, but other amusement parks that persist to this day suggest a different fate for memory. Traditional amusement parks like Kennywood stress memory because of its powerful connotations – the park is not simply an amusement landscape, it is a place where you met your wife; the wooden out-and-back roller coaster is not merely a ride, it is the place where you most vividly remember the outings with your family. Unlike other forms of popular culture that become memorable, the theme park ride and the theme park itself are connected to real experiences that are remembered in part due to the vivid associations of theming, landscaping, rides and attractions that dot the theme park landscape. Like the Greek 'method of loci', in which speakers memorized speeches by associating particular sections of a speech with specific memorable parts of a building or a town, the theme park builds associations between people and their lives and its iconic rides and architecture. The many critics of the theme park often forget that even in the face of their apparent artificiality theme parks are meaningful to people.

Numerous documentaries on the BBC in the United Kingdom and on channels like Discovery and Travel in the United States emphasize the meaning that is attached by people to theme parks. While many of these shows provide 'tips' to visitors on how best to experience a theme park, others express the delight that people have when they visit theme parks. Some people's connection to the theme park is so intense that they become engaged in one, or even marry. Novels and films offer interesting and often existential understandings of people and their theme parks. In the sentimental novel *The Five People You Meet in Heaven*, author Mitch Albom uses an amusement park, and its mechanic who struggles to grasp his worth in life, as the site of a Christian affirmation.[31] Though the mechanic's work may seem insignificant, he is brought to sacrifice himself and saves a little girl from a malfunctioning ride, expressing to the audience that even working at an amusement park can be noble, godly work. A less sentimental take on the theme park, Stanley Elkin's *The Magic Kingdom*, avoids the facile moralism of Ablom's.[32] Elkin's work centres on the theme park as a dual site of inspiration and tragedy. While in England, Elkin saw a news report about terminally ill boys who were being flown to Walt Disney World. The story became the inspiration for Elkin. He avoids the traditional approach of connecting the gravely ill children with the audience through feelings of sorrow by offering vivid and often troubling depictions of their physical and mental states. As many real-life examples illustrate, the theme park is a text that says, 'Use me as a way of dealing with your problems', but Elkin problematizes this image of the theme park and instead asks us to consider why these objects have taken on such obsessive yet meaningful places in our lives.[33] His presentation of the iconic landscapes of Walt Disney World as surreal and haunting places, and his juxtaposition of this imagery with the lives of these terribly ill children, offers a complex narrative of the theme park. Later works, like the teenage drama *Rollercoaster* (1999), use the theme park, in this case an abandoned one, as a site on which to project the most serious questions of life and on which they are potentially resolved.

Thus theme parks have a strong therapeutic role in society. People use theme parks as an escape from their often heavy, bored and conflicted lives. In the modern world and in the circumstances that Marshall Berman described (quoting Marx) as reflecting a condition in which 'all that is solid melts into air', theme parks provide a way to envision a world that never was and never could be; it is a world of fantasy that is 'virtual reality', a suspension of the reality outside the park's berm for the patron.[34] As one Disney animator said of the soothing function of Disney theme parks, 'People come here loaded with good intentions, but like all humans, they've brought two things with them: last week's hurt or pain, which they can't forget yet, and next month's payment or God knows what. So we overwhelm them . . . They forget tomorrow and they forget yesterday.'[35] Like a virtual reality space the theme park creates a new temporal and spatial order; it causes, as the animator suggests, a suspension of the day before and the day after; the only thing that matters while being in the theme park is that day itself, the time spent inside the park.

More recently theme parks have been represented as negative spaces within everyday life. In movies like *Final Destination 3* (2006), in which a group of teens tempt fate with a trip to a theme park, the thrill ride and the theme park become spaces of horror, asking us to rethink our gleeful mental images of the theme park. In fact, events like the Vietnam War, 9/11 and the war in Iraq illustrate how the horrors of the theme park can be played against the horrors of everyday life. Following 9/11 US President George W. Bush told Americans, 'We will not surrender our freedom to travel . . . And one of the great goals of this nation's war is to restore public confidence . . . Fly and enjoy America's great destination spots. Get down to Disney World in Florida. Take your families and enjoy life, the way we want it to be enjoyed.'[36] At the same time the US government notified its citizens that sites of tourism, including Disneyland and the Las Vegas Strip, were potential terrorist targets.[37] After 9/11 previously harmless videotapes showcasing the facade architecture of iconic casinos in Las Vegas or the many rides of Disneyland suddenly became sinister. In the United States' War on Terror, theme parks and themed spaces are redefined politically; they are not merely sites of amusement, they are terrorist targets because of their iconic status and because they represent American ideals of freedom, democracy and the free market. In a sense 'attendance at the parks serves as a proxy index of Americans' confidence in their own security'.[38] In the new American text Disneyland supplants Mount Rushmore, the Las Vegas Strip the Liberty Bell, and they symbolically take on greater value because of their possible status as targets of terrorism. The US government soon transformed Disneyland into a protected no-fly zone, not unlike spaces around Washington DC and nuclear power plants.[39] Disneyland and much of the Vegas Strip take on the quality of American sacred space that must be protected at all costs.[40] Likewise, the values of the nation, which are here directly expressed as the spatial forms of theme parks, casinos and other consumerist venues, are also upheld.

For some theme parks can become obsessions – an ultimate text that is written into their lives, their consciousness. I knew many workers at AstroWorld and a number of patrons who wanted to spend every day of their lives at the park. Some employees would come to the park on their day off and act like a patron might – experiencing all of the rides, attractions, shows and food from the other side. Theme park watchers and other aficionados (who are similar to football and other sports fans) use the theme park as a sounding board for life. While aboard a ride one can reflect on the ills that are not present in the suspended reality, while watching a show an individual can think of ways in which they feel connected to something bigger than themselves. If only for a day, while in a theme park the individual is given new meaning, new agency, a sense of being and belonging that contrasts with the harshness, alienation and discomfiting realities of the real world.

For loyal theme park employees and for theme park watchers the theme park offers a life text – a model for negotiating the world that promises to do much more than create an alternative reality fit for consumption. At many theme parks, including Six Flags AstroWorld, management provides theme park training that serves not only to inculcate in its workers the principles of effective guest service, efficiency and friendliness, but purports to change the very core of the worker – her soul. In theme park training programmes to which I was witness, workers were blindfolded on rides and, in powerful team-building simulations, people took turns attempting to safely get the riders to dismount the rides. In others, which approached the techniques of ritual, workers were passed on top of

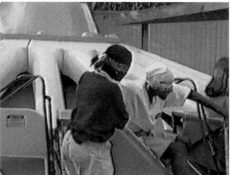

others, suggesting the idea of trusting the coworker even in the face of apparent risk. Members of management at the park saw it as their duty to do more than teach new employees their jobs; they wanted to affect people deeply, altering their inner cores in ways typically reserved for religion.[41] The same goal is present in the 'world as theme park': attraction managers, experiential space designers and proprietors of new third and lifestyle spaces envision altering people and society itself, all through the means of the new narrative of the theme park.

In its newest form the theme park presents a model for living, with the idea that it can transform workers and patrons alike as they go back into the real world and resume their normal lives, but this mission can have political consequences. On 6 August 1970 a group of Yippies invaded Disneyland. Their purpose was to spread their message of love and politics (and also critique the park's hair and grooming policies), while liberating Minnie Mouse and invading the spaces of the park. They laid siege to Tom Sawyer Island and even raised the Viet Cong flag on the island. Eventually the Los Angeles Police Department was called in to restore order, just before the park was closed for security reasons.[42] It is likely that

The theme park training programmes approximate the approaches of religion; their effect, it was hoped, was radically to alter both the worker and the person.

the Yippies chose Disneyland because of its connotations as a purveyor of straight society – as representing all that is clean, proper and apolitical. In September 2006 a similar but more subdued protest occurred at Disneyland. The artist Banksy covertly brought in an unlawful combatant detainee suit, similar to those worn at Guantanamo Bay, and inflated a dummy. Banksy placed the dummy outside Big Thunder Mountain Railroad where onlookers gawked at the spectacle.

Banksy's moment of protest was more shocking because of its location at the epicentre of popular culture consciousness. For many, the text that is Disneyland, and perhaps also the theme park, is a fantasy narrative that is removed from the political realities outside theme parks. By moving explicit politics inside the theme park both the Yippies and Banksy responded to the idea of there being no 'outside the text' of the theme park.[43] Since the United States invaded Iraq a number of critics have charged that the US has produced a 'terrorist Disneyland' in Iraq, a claim that further extends the interesting appropriations of the theme park as a text. In imagining Iraq as a terrorist Disneyland people are acknowledging both the expansion of the theme park model as a form in the world and the strange coalescence of fantasy and less ideal states like violence, danger and uncertainty.

In a moment of reducing the theme park to a purely political form, the performance artist Banksy smuggles a Guantanamo Bay-style orange detainee suit into Disneyland.

As a model for the world the theme park becomes a form and it impacts the world in four senses: it affects showing by instituting new spatial, architectural and geographic forms; it affects doing by structuring new models of the person, self and social relationships; it affects knowing in terms of its unique project of culture; and it affects telling by introducing new narratives that are used to understand the world. In terms of the first area, as theme parks have expanded throughout the world they bring with them new senses of how space and architecture can be constructed. Since the era of Coney Island theme parks have emphasized the juxtaposition of multiple forms, perspectives, visual modes and aesthetic techniques, often in the same or adjacent spaces. The form also teaches people how to clean up space, essentially working out the edges, kinks and imperfections and assuring that there is coherence between elements that may have otherwise been seen as distinct from one another. Theme parks also institute powerful control of perspective, gaze and the way in which an individual interprets space and architecture – without theme parks, our contemporary visual sensibilities would be radically different, if not dull. As a sum of showing, the theme park form creates the idea of absolute consumer space – an approach to construction that, like the city itself, affirms that all things can be in one place.

Like seeing, the form has a significant effect on how people do things in the world. Prior to the early amusement parks of Coney Island, people were less inclined to be comfortable mixing among the masses. The new form mixes people together with varying impacts, including new forms of sociality, new constructions of the self-other and the encouragement of new forms of tolerance (though sometimes emphasizing stereotypes). And throughout its history, as it has moved from the amusement park to the theme park, the form has shown an emphasis on altering the family and other kin relations. While the dynamic of how people are the focus of the theme park has changed – moving from the connection of people with many others to the contemporary trend of the isolated family – the theme park form has stressed a radical uprooting of the social order, striving for nothing less than changing the very core of people and their relations. In terms of work the theme park has introduced a new model of interaction, one based on dramaturgy and the idea of people playing parts in a social drama. Equally significant, the form evolves to impact the individual. Perhaps the most significant of all of the impacts, the theme park touches the individual, telling him that he is, ultimately, a part of the great show.

The theme park creates new spaces and new people, and it further shows itself as a fully fledged form in its operations on culture or ways of knowing. The ways people understand the world, including their senses of self and how they relate to others, are modified by the brands, logos, symbols and modes of consumerism that are endemic to the varied worlds of theme parks. As corporate models theme parks connect people to the world not through nature but through culture, specifically through forms of consumption. As a new vision of the world the theme park creates a unique canvas that connects multiple places, people, events and ideas in one confined space, and thus it condenses and interconnects cultures in ways previously unimaginable. Boldly, the form tells us that we can know the world through its essences: a particular look of a pagoda, a dance representative of a cultural group and a re-creation of a historical event. Whether we agree that such essentialism is valid or not, we recognize that knowing the world after the evolution of the theme park will never be the same. Also significant is the mode by which theme parks teach people about the world. Unlike a film in which the viewer watches and passively contemplates the world with two senses, in the theme park world the individual uses all the senses and understands that knowing is achieved through immersion, participation and seeing for oneself. Even museums, which have traditionally stressed austere forms of learning, have incorporated this important mode of knowing that is instituted by the form.

Lastly, the form creates a new approach to narrative and how ideas about the world are told. In a world that is prone to melting into air the theme park tells us that we can have completeness. Whereas people's relationships are characterized by disjuncture, their experiences by fragments and unexplained remainders, the theme park form institutes new powerful senses of the whole. In a theme park, and perhaps only in a theme park, people can once again have a feeling of being connected. As one moves from one ride to the next, into a restaurant and then into a gift shop, and even a restroom, one can feel that the whole is whole again: everything is connected to everything else through the marvel of theming. Telling also becomes dominated by new forms of technology that the theme park brings about. The multi-media attractions of these spaces let people know that there is magic in the world and, just like world's fairs did, theme parks suggest a prescient view of how the world might one day look. People are reassured that technology can save. The way narrative works in the theme park is through the monolithic perspective. Even though rides tell different stories and shops sell different products, the approach within any given theme park space is to control through the *one* perspective, the branded, corporate and optimistic one. Just as religions limit the space of narrative interpretation, the theme park form allows for a limited and powerful discourse about

the world. Perhaps most significant in how it alters telling is its introduction of new modes of interpretation – fantasy projections, upheaval of social norms, safety and reassurance – that, when combined, create an elixir more thought-inducing than the most powerful drugs.

In venues like Cabela's, located in the United States, the technologies of the theme park and their unique associated narratives are being deployed in uncanny ways. Cabela's retail stores combine traditional merchandise, extensive taxidermy displays, interactive video arcades, real-life archery ranges, giant aquariums, gun libraries, wild game eateries and a general store on a scale that had been previously possible only in theme parks. As Cabela's states in its own origin narrative, 'As much wildlife

At Cabela's the image of wildlife, mountain scenery, and consumer society merge.

museums and education centers as retail stores, Cabela's showrooms provide a truly unique shopping experience'.[44] At many of the stores, a featured Conservation Mountain provides a stunning backdrop for the consumerism that takes place throughout the stores. Stuffed elk, grizzly bears, elephants, tigers and other big game roam motionless on mountains above customers who gleefully snap pictures and take videos as if they were participating in a real-life safari. Many parents use Cabela's to teach their children about the fauna that, ironically, are killed by the weapons and technologies available for purchase on numerous shelves and tables throughout the store. Clearly, the stakes of contemporary society have changed, as has the nature of the theme park, and the question is no longer *what* is being taught and sold but *how* it is being taught and sold.

Cabela's illustrates how the approaches of the theme park can be modified and applied in ways that comfort patrons. The newest theme parks act as powerful lifespaces – as physical places that project educational, political, and lifestyle messages amidst all the consumerism. Like the Paleolithic caves and the real mountains of prehistory that contained some of the species represented in these stores, Cabela's provides a fully functioning space that fulfills both utilitarian and symbolic needs. In their final moments as a form, just before they are likely transformed into hybrid and virtual objects, theme parks aim to teach. They know that we may be too busy to read a book or too cynical to watch CNN, so they aim to convince us through their immensely powerful materiality and immersion. We approach them, cautiously, but something about their recreated facades, however superfluous they seem, draws us to them. We take them, touch them, make them a part of us, and we offer something back to them, giving them life. Like our early human ancestors who may have used symbolic caves to deal with the unrealities, the difficulties, of the real world, we use these virtual spaces to do much the same. Today, the stakes have changed, as have the stresses of everyday life, but the theme park, like the utilitarian and symbolic forms of the past, provides people across the world with a way out of life and a uniquely new way of life. With their varied fantasy projections, theme parks will, no doubt, continue to thrill and enrage us.

References

Preface

1 Judith Rubin, '2006 Theme Park Attendance Numbers Demonstrate the Benefits of Reinvestment', Burbank, CA: TEA, 2007, www.themeit.com/attendance_report2006.pdf (accessed 15 January 2008).

2 Duncan Kennedy, 'Mexico's "Migrant Mountain"', BBC News Mexico, www.news.bbc.co.uk/2/hi/programmes/from_our_own_correspondent/6390297.stm (accessed 15 January 2008).

3 Kathleen Kingsbury, 'Postcard: Shenzhen', *TIME* (10 December 2007), p. 8.

4 For more on Huis Ten Bosch see Marc Treib, 'Theme Park, Themed Living: The Case of Huis Ten Bosch [Japan]', in Terence Young and Robert Riley, eds, *Theme Park Landscapes: Antecedents and Variations* (Washington, DC, 2002). Miodrag Mitrasinovic, *Total Landscape, Theme Parks, Public Space* (Burlington, VT, 2006)

5 Jean-François Lyotard, *The Postmodern Condition: A Report on Knowledge* (Minneapolis, MN, 1991), p. 76.

6 Scott A. Lukas, 'The Hummer as Cultural and Political Myth: A Multi-Sited Ethnographic Analysis', in Elaine Cardenas and Ellen Gorman, eds, *The Hummer: Myths and Consumer Culture* (Lanham, MD, 2007).

7 Siegfried Kracauer, 'The Mass Ornament', in Anton Kaes, Martin Jay and Edward Dimendberg, eds, *The Weimar Republic Sourcebook* (Berkeley, CA, 1994), pp. 404–7.

1 Theme Park as Oasis

1 Maxim Gorky, 'Boredom', *The Independent* (8 August 1907), p. 312.

2 *Oxford English Dictionary*, second edn (Broadbridge, Alderley, Wotton-under-Edge, 1989).

3 Louis Wasserman, *Merchandising Architecture: Architectural Implications and Applications of Amusement Themeparks* (Sheboygan, WI, 1978), p. 51. For more on the history of pleasure gardens see Warwick William Wroth, *The London Pleasure Gardens of the Eighteenth Century* (New York, 1896).

4 William F. Mangels, *The Outdoor Amusement Industry: From Earliest Times to the Present* (New York, 1952), p. 6.

5 *Ibid.*, p. 7.

6 Judith A. Adams, *The American Amusement Park Industry* (Boston, MA, 1991), p. 6.

7 Mangels, *The Outdoor Amusement Industry*, p. 6.

8 Heath Schenker, 'Pleasure Gardens, Theme Parks, and the Picturesque', in Terence Young and Robert Riley, eds, *Theme Park Landscapes: Antecedents and Variations* (Washington, DC, 2002), p. 74.

9 Mangels, *The Outdoor Amusement Industry*, p. 9.

10 Norman Klein, *The Vatican to Vegas: A History of Special Effects* (New York, 2004).

11 Adams, *The American Amusement Park Industry*, p. 7.

12 *Ibid.*

13 Wasserman, *Merchandising Architecture*, p. 52.

14 Edo McCullough, *Good Old Coney Island: A Sentimental Journey into the Past* (New York, 2000), p. 195. At Steeplechase Tilyou believed that 'infinite variety' was the order of the day, *ibid.*, p. 309.

15 Walter Benjamin, 'Grandville, or the World Exhibitions', in *Reflections* (New York, 1978), p. 152.

16 Neil Harris, 'Great American Fairs and American Cities: The Role of Chicago's Columbian Exposition', in *Cultural Excursions: Marketing Appetites and Cultural Tastes in Modern America* (Chicago, IL, 1990), p. 126.

17 *Ibid.*, p. 123.

18 See Adams, *The American Amusement Park Industry*, p. 21.

19 Umberto Eco, 'A Theory of Expositions', in *Travels in Hyperreality* (San Diego, CA, 1983), p. 299.

20 *Official Guidebook, New York World's Fair 1939* (New York, 1939), p. 37.

21 *Ibid.*, p. 40.

22 *Ibid.*, p. 72.

23 See Woody Register, *The Kid of Coney Island: Fred Thompson and the Rise of American Amusements* (Oxford, 2001), pp. 69–73. I would like to acknowledge Dr Register's helpful responses to my questions regarding Fred Thompson and the Trip to the Moon attraction.

24 Harris, 'Great American Fairs and American Cities', p. 129.

25 Ric Burns, *Coney Island: The American Experience* (PBS documentary film, 2000). Transcript available at www.pbs.org/wgbh/amex/coney/filmmore/transcript /index.html (accessed 15 January 2008).

26 McCullough, *Good Old Coney Island*, p. 56.

27 Gary Kyriazi, *The Great American Amusement Parks: A Pictorial History* (Secaucus, NJ, 1978), p. 31.

28 Quoted in Michael Immerso, *Coney Island: The People's Playground* (New Brunswick, NJ, 2002), p. 41.

29 Immerso, *Coney Island*, p. 46.

30 Burns, *Coney Island*.

31 McCullough, *Good Old Coney Island*, p. 299.

32 *Ibid.*

33 Albert Bigelow Paine, 'The New Coney Island', *Century Illustrated Magazine*, LXVIII/4 (August 1904), p. 537.

34 Kyriazi, *The Great American Amusement Parks*, p. 44.

35 McCullough, *Good Old Coney Island*, p. 286.

36 Reginald Wright Kauffman, 'What Is Coney?', *Hampton's Magazine*, XXIII (August 1909), p. 224.

37 John F. Kasson, *Amusing the Million: Coney Island at the Turn of the Century* (New York, 1978), p. 59.

38 Burns, *Coney Island*.

39 Immerso, *Coney Island*, p. 62.

40 Register, *The Kid of Coney Island*, p. 86. It has also been suggested that Luna's naming owes something to Skip Dundy's sister, Luna. Oliver Pilat and Jo Ranson, *Sodom By the Sea: An Affectionate History of Coney Island* (Garden City, NY, 1941), p. 146.

41 Quoting Richard Snow in David Nasaw, *Going Out: The Rise and Fall of Public Amusements* (New York, 1993), p. 83.

42 For a detailed discussion of Fred Thompson, see Register, *The Kid of Coney Island*.

43 Frederick [*sic*] A. Thompson, 'The Summer Show', *The Independent* (20 June 1907), p. 1461.

44 Quoting historian Chester H. Liebs, Register, *The Kid of Coney Island*, p. 53.

45 *Ibid.*, pp. 53–4.

46 Rem Koolhaas, 'Coney Island: The Technology of the Fantastic', in *Delirious New York* (New York, 1994), p. 38.

47 Bruce Bliven, 'Coney Island for Battered Souls', *The New Republic* (23 November 1921), p. 372.

48 Register, *The Kid of Coney Island*, p. 83.

49 Frederic Thompson, 'Amusing People', *Metropolitan*, XXXII (August 1910), p. 601.

50 Thompson, 'The Summer Show', pp. 1460–61.

51 Register, *The Kid of Coney Island*, pp. 8, 98.

52 Adams, *The American Amusement Park Industry*, p. 48.

53 John S. Berman, *Coney Island* (New York, 2003), p. 35.

54 Register, *The Kid of Coney Island*, p. 131.

55 Immerso, *Coney Island*, p. 74.

56 *Ibid.*, p. 71.

57 Koolhaas, 'Coney Island', p. 46.

58 Kyriazi, *The Great American Amusement Parks*, pp. 71–2.

59 Koolhaas, 'Coney Island', p. 45.

60 Immerso, *Coney Island*, p. 83.

61 Burns, *Coney Island*.

1 Stephen F. Mills, *The American Landscape* (Edinburgh, 1997), p. 1.
2 Yi-Fu Tuan, *Topophilia: A Study of Environmental Perception, Attitudes, and Values* (New York, 1990), p. 11.
3 Scott A. Lukas, 'The Themed Space: Locating Culture, Nation, and Self', in Scott A. Lukas, ed., *The Themed Space: Locating Culture, Nation, and Self* (Lanham, MD, 2007), p. 1.
4 Terence Young, 'Grounding the Myth – Theme Park Landscapes in an Era of Commerce and Nationalism', in Terence Young and Robert Riley, eds, *Theme Park Landscapes: Antecedents and Variations* (Washington, DC, 2002), p. 6.
5 Anthony Iannacci, ed., *Gensler Entertainment: The Art of Placemaking* (New York, 2001), p. 5.
6 David Lowenthal, 'The Past as a Theme Park', in Young and Riley, *Theme Park Landscapes*, p. 18.
7 *Disney Vacation Planner* 2002 and *Disney Vacation Planner* 1995 (both on video).
8 Tony Bennett, *The Birth of the Museum* (London, 1995), pp. 60–61.
9 New York World's Fair *Official Guidebook*, p. 40.
10 *Ibid.*
11 *Ibid.*, p. 44.
12 *Ibid.*, pp. 45–73
13 John M. Findlay, 'Disneyland: The Happiest Place on Earth', in *Magic Lands: Western Cityscapes and American Culture After 1940* (Berkeley, CA, 1992), p. 66.
14 See Richard V. Francaviglia, *Main Street Revisited: Time, Space, and Image Building in Small-Town America* (Iowa City, IA, 1996).
15 The Imagineers, *Walt Disney Imagineering: A Behind the Dreams Look at Making the Magic Real* (New York, 1996), p. 84.
16 *Ibid.*
17 See Karal Ann Marling, 'Imagineering the Disney Theme Parks', in Karal Ann Marling, ed., *Designing Disney's Theme Parks: The Architecture of Reassurance* (Paris, 1997), pp. 43–7.
18 Findlay, 'Disneyland', p. 58.
19 Quoting Hill, Findlay, 'Disneyland', p. 66.
20 Findlay, 'Disneyland', p. 65.
21 *Six Flags Employee Handbook*, 1994, p. 1, sec. 3.
22 Gary Kyriazi, *The Great American Amusement Parks: A Pictorial History* (Secaucus, NJ, 1978), p. 182.
23 *Ibid.*, p. 183.
24 One of the best historical websites that offers a glimpse of Freedomland is 'Welcome to Freedomland USA', www.ourworld.compuserve.com/homepages /robfriedman/ (accessed 15 January 2008).
25 Window on China press kit, 1993.
26 Scott A. Lukas, 'A Politics of Reverence and Irreverence: Social Discourse on

Theming Controversies', in Lukas, *The Themed Space*, p. 273.

27 Hai Ren, 'The Landscape of Power: Imagineering Consumer Behavior at China's Theme Parks', in Lukas, *The Themed Space*. I am indebted to Hai Ren's remarkable work on Chinese theme parks, much of which will be reflected in his forthcoming book on the subject. See also Nick Stanley, 'Chinese Theme Parks and National Identity', in Young and Riley, *Theme Park Landscapes*.

28 One of its press releases makes this claim, as the 'nation's first theme park'. Holiday World, 'From Santa Claus Land to Holiday World: 61 Years of Family Fun', 2007, www.holidayworld.com (accessed 15 January 2008).

29 Holiday World, 'More Family Rides', www.holidayworld.com/more_family_ rides.html (accessed 15 January 2008).

30 See Lukas, 'A Politics of Reverence and Irreverence'.

31 Universal Orlando, 'Compare to Disney', www.universalorlando.com/disney_ comparision.html (accessed 15 January 2008).

32 Universal Orlando, 'Two Amazing Theme Parks Two Completely Different Experiences!', www.universalorlando.com/parks_overview.html (accessed 15 January 2008).

33 Lyotard offered one of the most apt definitions of postmodern culture, 'Eclecticism is the degree zero of contemporary general culture: one listens to reggae, watches a western, eats McDonald's food for lunch and local cuisine for dinner, wears Paris perfume in Tokyo and "retro" clothes in Hong Kong; knowledge is a matter for TV games'. *The Postmodern Condition*, (Minneapolis, MN, 1991), p. 76.

34 Michael Sorkin, 'See You in Disneyland', in Michael Sorkin, ed., *Variations on a Theme Park* (New York, 1992).

35 Dollywood, 'Heritage and Crafts', www.dollywood.com/heritage-crafts (accessed 15 January 2008).

36 Dollywood, 'Shows', www.dollywood.com/shows (accessed 15 January 2008).

37 See Melissa Jane Hardie, 'Torque: Dollywood, Pigeon Forge, and Authentic Feeling in the Smoky Mountains', in Lukas, *The Themed Space*.

38 See Peter Adey, '"Above Us Only Sky": Themes, Simulations, and Liverpool John Lennon Airport', in Lukas, *The Themed Space*.

39 Scott A. Lukas, 'Key Terms', in Lukas, *The Themed Space*, p. 296.

40 Sharon Zukin, 'Learning from Disney World', in *The Culture of Cities* (Malden, MA, 1995), p. 49.

41 John F. Kasson, *Amusing the Million: Coney Island at the Turn of the Century* (New York, 1978), p. 8.

42 Margaret J. King, 'The New American Muse: Notes on the Amusement/Theme Park', *Journal of Popular Culture*, XV/1, p. 59.

3 Theme Park as Machine

1 Quoted in Richard Munch, *Harry G. Traver: Legends of Terror* (Fairview Park, OH, 1994), p. 137.
2 William F. Mangels, *The Outdoor Amusement Industry: From Earliest Times to the Present* (New York, 1952), p. 58.
3 *Ibid.*, p. 66.
4 *Ibid.*, p. 57.
5 For more on theme parks as landscapes of motion see Brenda J. Brown, 'Landscapes of Theme Park Rides: Media, Modes, Messages', in Terence Young and Robert Riley, eds, *Theme Park Landscapes: Antecedents and Variations* (Washington, DC, 2002).
6 Tony Bennett, *The Birth of the Museum* (London, 1995), p. 238. In the quote Bennett is referring specifically to Blackpool.
7 Larry Bleiberg, 'One Day, 41 Rides: It's No Problem for the Line King', *San Francisco Chronicle* (11 March 2007).
8 Herma Silverstein, *Scream Machines: Roller Coasters Past, Present, and Future* (New York, 1986), p. 7. Another significant source on the history of the roller coaster is Robert Cartmell, *The Incredible Scream Machine: A History of the Roller Coaster* (Fairview Park, OH, 1988).
9 Silverstein, *Scream Machines*, p. 10.
10 *Ibid.*, p. 11.
11 Todd H. Throgmorton, *Roller Coasters of America* (Osceola, WI, 1994), p. 37.
12 Munch, *Harry G. Traver*, p. 79.
13 *Ibid.*, p. 81.
14 One of the most famous cases of contemporary roller coaster injury occurred on the Rattler at Six Flags Fiesta Texas. Over 250 cases were filed as a result of injuries largely sustained from the first drop. In response, the ride was modified – tamed – which resulted in complaints from riders who preferred the harder ride. See www.rideaccidents.com/rattler.html (accessed 15 January 2008).
15 Munch, *Harry G. Traver*, p. 17.
16 Jean Baudrillard, *The System of Objects* (London, 1996), p. 115.
17 Quoted in the video *Wild Rides* 1997 (Discovery Channel).
18 *CNN*, 'Taking the Plunge', www.cnn.com/TRAVEL/DESTINATIONS/9706/roller. coasters/weddings.html (accessed 15 January 2008).
19 Tim Onosko, *Funland USA* (New York, 1978), p. 59.
20 For more on the roller coaster as an architectural symbol, see J. Meredith Neil, 'The Roller Coaster: Architectural Symbol and Sign', *Journal of Popular Culture*, XV/1.
21 Custom Coasters President Denise Larrick quoted in *Wild Rides* 1997 (Discovery Channel).
22 Paul L. Ruben, quoted in Larry Gerber 'Magic Mountain's Record-Speed Ride Reflects New Roller Coaster "Arms Race"', *Daily News* (Los Angeles) (15 May 1996).

23 For more on ride accidents see the comprehensive website, www.rideaccidents.com (accessed 15 January 2008).

24 Lewis Mumford, *Technics and Civilization* (New York, 1934), p. 426.

25 See Scott A. Lukas, 'The Theme Park and the Figure of Death', *Interculture*, II/2 (2005), www.iph.fsu.edu/interculture/pdfs/lukas%20theme%20park%20death.pdf and Ride Accidents, www.rideaccidents.com (accessed 15 January 2008).

26 Ulrich Beck, *Risk Society: Towards a New Modernity* (London, 1992). For a focus on the role of fire-fighting and risk-based disasters at Coney Island, see Lynn Sally, 'Luna Park's Fantasy World and Dreamland's White City: Fire Spectacles at Coney Island as Elemental Performativity', in Scott A. Lukas, ed., *The Themed Space: Locating Culture, Nation, and Self* (Lanham, MD, 2007).

27 Another is of paedophile workers. Peter Schweizer and Rochelle Schweizer, 'Disney's Pedophile Problem', in *Disney: The Mouse Betrayed* (Washington, DC, 1998), pp. 75–93.

28 Stephen M. Fjellman, *Vinyl Leaves: Walt Disney World and America* (Boulder, CO, 1992), p. 386.

29 *Fun House* (Discovery Channel documentary film, 1997).

30 Edwin Slosson, 'The Amusement Business', *The Independent* (21 July 1904), pp. 135–6.

31 John F. Kasson, *Amusing the Million: Coney Island at the Turn of the Century* (New York, 1978), p. 59.

32 Slosson, 'The Amusement Business', p. 139.

33 Frederick [*sic*] A. Thompson, 'The Summer Show', *The Independent* (20 June 1907), p. 1463.

34 Kennywood, www.kennywood.com. On December 11, 2007, it was announced that Kennywood was sold to a major theme park company, Parques Reunidos, a company that manages 61 other parks. According to a Kennywood press release, 'The Kennywood experience – as visitors have come to love and expect – will continue. Nothing will seem different'. See, 'New Chapter in Kennywood Entertainment History Announced', www.kennywood.com/docs/12.11.07KECNewChapterRelease.pdf (accessed 15 January 2008).

4 Theme Park as Show

1 Quoted in Johan Huizinga, *Homo Ludens: A Study of the Play Element in Culture* (Boston, MA, 1967), pp. 18–19.

2 Michael Brick, 'And Next to the Bearded Lady, Premature Babies', *New York Times* (12 June 2005).

3 John F. Kasson, *Amusing the Million: Coney Island at the Turn of the Century* (New York, 1978), p. 8.

4 Huizinga, *Homo Ludens*, p. 45.

5 Roger Caillois, *Man, Play and Games* (Champaign, IL, 2001), pp. 25–6.

6 Robert Venturi, Denise Scott Brown and Steven Izenour, *Learning From Las Vegas: The Forgotten Symbolism of Architectural Form*, revd edn (Cambridge, MA, 1993).

7 Rem Koolhaas and Hans Ulrich Obrist, 'Re-learning from Las Vegas', interview with Denise Scott Brown and Robert Venturi, in Rem Koolhaas, ed., *Content* (Cologne, 2004), p. 150.

8 Quoted in Giovanna Franci, *Dreaming of Italy: Las Vegas and the Virtual Grand Tour* (Reno, NV, 2005), p. 118.

9 Jean Baudrillard, *The Perfect Crime* (London, 1996), n.p.

10 Roland Barthes, *Camera Lucida: Reflections on Photography* (New York, 1981), pp. 26–7

11 The Imagineers, *Walt Disney Imagineering: A Behind the Dreams Look at Making the Magic Real* (New York, 1996), p. 84.

12 *Luna Park: The Electric City By the Sea* (Brooklyn, NY, 1903), p. 5.

13 For more on uncontrollable animals see Jason Hribal, 'When Animals Resist Their Exploitation: Kasatka, the Sea World Orca', *CounterPunch* (14 December 2006), www.counterpunch.org/hribal12142006.html (accessed 15 January 2008).

14 The Imagineers, *The Imagineering Field Guide to Disney's Animal Kingdom* (New York, 2007), p. 17.

15 *Ibid.*, p. 16.

16 *Ibid.*, p. 18.

17 Susan G. Davis, *Spectacular Nature: Corporate Culture and the Sea World* [sic] *Experience* (Berkeley, CA, 1997).

18 Frontline, *A Whale of a Business* (PBS documentary film, 1997), www.pbs.org/wgbh/pages/frontline/shows/whales/seaworld (accessed 15 January 2008).

19 Kasson, *Amusing the Million*, p. 23.

20 *Ibid.*

21 *Oxford English Dictionary*, www.dictionary.oed.com, second edn (Broadbridge, Alderley, Wotton-under-Edge, 1989).

22 Kasson, *Amusing the Million*, p. 82. See also Frederic Thompson, 'Amusing the Million', *Everybody's Magazine* (19 September 1908), pp. 378–86.

23 Jean McFaddin, 'Thinking Big', in David Rockwell, ed., *Spectacle* (London, 2006), p. 50.

24 Hai Ren, 'The Landscape of Power: Imagineering Consumer Behavior at China's Theme Parks', in Scott A. Lukas, ed., *The Themed Space: Locating Culture, Nation, and Self* (Lanham, MD, 2007), p. 106.

25 Standinaqueue, www.standinaqueue.wordpress.com (accessed 15 January 2008).

26 See Stephen M. Fjellman, *Vinyl Leaves: Walt Disney World and America* (Boulder, CO, 1992), pp. 205–9.

27 Jim Fitzgerald, 'Disney Plays Tricks with Mickey Mouse Lines', *Bellevue (Michigan) Gazette* (2 May 1984).

28 For more on the issue of people being drawn into the ride narrative see The Project on Disney, 'Story Time', in *Inside the Mouse: Work and Play at Disney World* (Durham, NC, 1995), pp. 79–81 and Scott Bukatman, 'There's Always

Tomorrowland: Disney and the Hypercinematic Experience', *October*, LVII (Summer 1991), p. 60.

29 Scott A. Lukas, 'How the Theme Park Gets Its Power: Lived Theming, Social Control, and the Themed Worker Self', in Lukas, *The Themed Space*, p. 187.

30 The Imagineers, *Walt Disney Imagineering*, p. 11.

31 Bill Capodagli and Lynn Jackson, *The Disney Way: Harnessing the Management Secrets of Disney in Your Company* (New York, 1999), p. 133.

32 See Lukas, 'How the Theme Park Gets Its Power'.

33 Paul Goldberger, 'Architecture View; 25 Years of Unabashed Elitism', *New York Times* (2 February 1992).

34 David Koenig, *Mouse Tales: A Behind-the-Ears Look at Disneyland* (Irvine, CA, 1994), p. 209.

35 Ann Brigham, 'Behind-the-Scenes Spaces: Promoting Production in a Land of Consumption', in Lukas, *The Themed Space*.

36 Scott A. Lukas, 'An American Theme Park: Working and Riding Out Fear in the Late Twentieth Century', in George E. Marcus, ed., *Late Editions 6, Paranoia within Reason: A Casebook on Conspiracy as Explanation* (Chicago, IL, 1999).

37 Woody Register, *The Kid of Coney Island: Fred Thompson and the Rise of American Amusements* (Oxford, 2001), p. 100.

38 Dickens World, 'Great Expectations for Dickens World' (May 2007), www.dickensworld.co.uk/index.php?option=com_content&task=blogcategory&id=2 3&Itemid=45 (accessed 15 January 2008).

39 'What the Dickens?', *Guardian* (18 April 2007), www.books.guardian.co.uk/ departments/classics/story/0,,2059804,00.html (accessed 15 January 2008).

40 Dickens World, 'Great Expectations for Dickens World'.

41 Lawrence Pollard, 'Learning English – Words in the News: Dickens World', BBC (25 May 2007), www.bbc.co.uk/worldservice/learningenglish/newsenglish/witn/ 2007/05/070528_dickens.shtml (accessed 15 January 2008).

42 The Victorian Peeper (21 April 2007), www.victorianpeeper.blogspot.com/2007/04/ dickens-world-revealed.html (accessed 15 January 2008).

43 Edwin Slosson, 'The Amusement Business', *The Independent* (21 July 1904), p. 139.

44 On the significance of the patron's role in new experiential spaces, see Brian Lonsway, 'The Experience of a Lifestyle', in Lukas, *The Themed Space*.

45 For more on the theming of Las Vegas, see Scott A. Lukas, 'Theming as a Sensory Phenomenon: Discovering the Senses on the Las Vegas Strip', in Lukas, *The Themed Space* and Scott A. Lukas, 'The Theming of Everyday Life: Mapping the Self, Life Politics, and Cultural Hegemony on the Las Vegas Strip', *Community College Humanities Review* 27 (Fall 2006–7).

1 Guy Debord, *The Society of the Spectacle* (New York, 1994), p. 12.
2 John M. Findlay, 'Disneyland: The Happiest Place on Earth', in *Magic Lands: Western Cityscapes and American Culture After 1940* (Berkeley, CA, 1992), p. 70.
3 *Oxford English Dictionary*, second edn (Broadbridge, Alderley, Wotton-under-Edge, 1989).
4 Edo McCullough, *Good Old Coney Island: A Sentimental Journey into the Past* (New York, 2000), p. 311.
5 See 'A Tale of Two Tillies', www.mistersnitch.blogspot.com/2005/08/tale-of-two-tillies.html (accessed 15 January 2008).
6 Sharon Zukin, 'Learning from Disney World', in *The Culture of Cities* (Malden, MA, 1995), p. 58.
7 The Project on Disney, 'Story Time', in *Inside the Mouse: Work and Play at Disney World* (Durham, NC, 1995), p. 192.
8 Martin Lindstrom, 'A Brand Theme Park for Children: Kidzania's Unique Style of "Edutainment"', *Advertising Age*, 23 April 2007, www.adage.com (accessed 15 January 2008).
9 Chris Betros, 'Kids' Night Out', *Metropolis* (10 November 2006), www.metropolis.co.jp/tokyo/659/feature.asp (accessed 15 January 2008).
10 Henry A. Giroux, *The Mouse that Roared: Disney and the End of Innocence* (Lanham, MD, 1999), p. 17.
11 Chris Betros, 'Kids' Night Out'.
12 Giroux, *The Mouse that Roared*, p. 19.
13 Umberto Eco, 'A Theory of Expositions', in *Travels in Hyperreality* (San Diego, CA, 1983), p. 296.
14 Barbara Rubin, 'Aesthetic Ideology and Urban Design', *Annals of the Association of American Geographers*, LXIX/3 (1979), p. 349.
15 John F. Kasson, *Amusing the Million: Coney Island at the Turn of the Century* (New York, 1978), p. 15.
16 Scott A. Lukas, 'How the Theme Park Gets Its Power: Lived Theming, Social Control, and the Themed Worker Self', in Scott A. Lukas, ed., *The Themed Space: Locating Culture, Nation, and Self* (Lanham, MD, 2007).
17 Richard E. Foglesong, *Married to the Mouse: Walt Disney World and Orlando* (New Haven, CT, 2001).
18 *Disney: Time & Again*, NBC documentary film.
19 Findlay, 'Disneyland', p. 106.
20 *Ibid.*, p. 67.
21 Jean Baudrillard, *Simulations* (New York, 1983), p. 25.
22 Adam Davidson, 'Keepers of the Magic Kingdom', *LA Weekly* (4 September 2003).
23 Kevin Roberts, *Lovemarks: The Future Beyond Brands* (New York, 2004).
24 *Ibid.*, p. 79.
25 *Ibid.*, p. 77.

26 For more on the specifics of theme park-cinema intertextuality see Anne Friedberg, *Window Shopping: Cinema and the Postmodern* (Berkeley, CA, 1993), pp. 89–90, and Scott A. Lukas, 'The Cinematic Theme Park', unpublished.

27 The video was removed in December 2007 due to copyright issues.

28 For more, see Theme Park Review's photos, www.themeparkreview.com/japan2004/nara1.htm (accessed 15 January 2008).

29 Judith A. Adams, *The American Amusement Park Industry* (Boston, 1991), p. 67.

30 Universal Orlando, 'Harry Potter to Cast Spell on Universal Orlando Resort' (31 May 2007), www.media.universalorlando.com/harrypotter (accessed 15 January 2008).

31 Stephen Brown, 'Harry Potter: Brand Wizard', Brandchannel.com (18 July 2005), www.brandchannel.com/features_profile.asp?pr_id=241 (accessed 15 January 2008).

32 Universal Orlando, 'Harry Potter to Cast Spell on Universal Orlando Resort'.

33 Frontline, *A Whale of a Business* (PBS documentary film, 1997), www.pbs.org/wgbh/pages/frontline/shows/whales/seaworld (accessed 15 January 2008).

34 *Ibid.*

35 George Ritzer, *Enchanting a Disenchanted World: Revolutionizing the Means of Consumption* (Thousand Oaks, CA, 1999), p. 6.

36 See Melissa Jane Hardie, 'Torque: Dollywood, Pigeon Forge, and Authentic Feeling in the Smoky Mountains', in Lukas, *The Themed Space*.

37 John Harlow, 'Screaming Rollercoaster Will Kick Off Bruce Lee Theme Park', *The Sunday Times* (3 September 2006), www.timesonline.co.uk/tol/news/world/article626516.ece (accessed 15 January 2008).

38 See Peter Adey, '"Above Us Only Sky": Themes, Simulations, and Liverpool John Lennon Airport', in Lukas, *The Themed Space*.

39 Legoland, 'Explore Village', www.legoland.com/park/parkoverview/explorevillage.htm (accessed 15 January 2008).

40 Robert Scally, 'Legoland Retail Theme Park Strives for "Big" Brand Image', *Discount Store News* (5 April 1999).

41 Matthew Brown, 'Abu Dhabi to Build Ferrari Theme Park on Island', Bloomberg.com (29 November 2006), www.bloomberg.com/apps/news?pid=20601093&refer=home&sid=alOwOksSfYsY (accessed 15 January 2008).

42 Hard Rock, 'Hard Rock Announces Plans for a Unique Rock n' Roll Theme Park' (31 March 2006), www.hrpusa.com/press1.html (accessed 15 January 2008).

43 Tux Turkel, 'Bean Sees Theme Park on Horizon', *Portland Press Herald* (5 June 2007).

44 *Le Monde*, www.jcdurbant.blog.lemonde.fr/2006/07/02/2006_07_mickey_go_home_ (accessed 15 January 2008).

45 Andrew Lainsbury, *Once Upon an American Dream: The Story of Euro Disneyland* (Lawrence, KS, 2000).

46 Aviad E. Raz, *Riding the Black Ship: Japan and Tokyo Disneyland* (Cambridge, MA, 1999), p. 3.

47 Disney designer John Hench, in Patricia Leigh Brown, 'In Fairy Dust, Disney Finds New Realism', *New York Times* (20 July 1989).

48 See Michael R. Solomon, 'The Store as Theme Park', in *Conquering Consumerspace: Marketing Strategies for a Branded World* (Boston, 2003), p. 166.

49 Paul Goldberger, 'The Store Strikes Back', *New York Times* (6 April 1997).

50 *Ibid.*

51 'The World's Largest Indoor Water Park: Seagaia Ocean Dome, Miyazaki', *Japan News Review* (5 June 2007), www.japannewsreview.com/travel/20070605page_id=71 (accessed 15 January 2008).

52 Tropical Islands, www.tropical-islands.de/en.html (accessed 15 January 2008).

53 *Ibid.*

54 Zukin, 'Learning from Disney World', p. 52.

55 South China Mall, www.southchinamall.com.cn/english/index1.jsp (accessed 15 January 2008).

56 Scott A. Lukas, 'Theming as a Sensory Phenomenon: Discovering the Senses on the Las Vegas Strip', in Lukas, *The Themed Space*.

57 See Ray Oldenburg, *The Great Good Place: Cafes, Coffee Shops, Bookstores, Bars, Hair Salons, and Other Hangouts at the Heart of a Community* (New York, 1999) and Ray Oldenburg, *Celebrating the Third Place: Inspiring Stories About the 'Great Good Places' at the Heart of Our Communities* (New York, 2002).

58 Findlay, 'Disneyland', p. 70.

59 Project for Public Spaces, www.pps.org/info/placemakingtools/placemakers/jhkunstler (accessed 15 January 2008). See also James Howard Kunstler, *The Geography of Nowhere: The Rise And Decline of America's Man-Made Landscape* (New York, 1994).

60 T. D. Allman, 'The Theme-Parking, Megachurching, Franchising, Exurbing, McMansioning of America: How Walt Disney Changed Everything', *National Geographic* (March 2007), www.ngm.nationalgeographic.com/ngm/0703/feature4 (accessed 15 January 2008).

61 Naomi Klein, *No Logo* (New York, 1999), p. 155.

62 Andrew Ross, *The Celebration Chronicles: Life, Liberty, and the Pursuit of Property Value in Disney's New Town* (New York, 1999).

63 Zygmunt Bauman, *Consuming Life* (Cambridge, 2007), p. 6.

64 See also Robert D. Putnam, *Bowling Alone: The Collapse and Revival of American Community* (New York, 2001).

6 Theme Park as Text

1 Jean Baudrillard, *The System of Objects* (London, 1996), p. 117.

2 Anand Giridharadas, 'In India, a Café Named Hitler's Cross', *International Herald Tribune* (28 August 2006).

3 *Ibid.*

4 *Ibid.*

5 For more on these controversial themed spaces, see Scott A. Lukas, 'A Politics of

Reverence and Irreverence: Social Discourse on Theming Controversies', in Scott
A. Lukas, ed., *The Themed Space: Locating Culture, Nation, and Self* (Lanham,
MD, 2007).

6 George Saunders, *Pastoralia* (New York, 2000).

7 George Saunders, *Civilwarland in Bad Decline* (New York, 1997).

8 George Lakoff and Mark Johnson, *Metaphors We Live By* (Chicago, 1980), p. 10.
The concept is associated with the work of Michael Reddy.

9 Alan E. Bryman, *The Disneyization of Society* (London, 2004), p. 1.

10 *Ibid.*, p. 2.

11 Clifford Geertz, 'Deep Play: Notes on the Balinese Cockfight', in *The Interpretation
of Cultures* (New York, 1973).

12 Robert Stuart Nathan, *Amusement Park* (New York, 1977); Lincoln Child, *Utopia*
(New York, 2002); Michael Crichton, *Jurassic Park* (New York, 2006).

13 Richard D. Land and Frank D. York, *Send a Message to Mickey* (Nashville, TN,
1998), back cover.

14 Kimi Yoshino, 'From Ashes to Ashes, at Disneyland', *Los Angeles Times*
(14 November 2007).

15 Some of these park ghost tales are detailed on www.ghostchatter.com/
ghsparchives/hauntedpark.htm (accessed 15 January 2008).

16 For more on these specific tales see www.unexplainable.net/artman/publish/
article_3256.shtml (accessed 15 January 2008).

17 David Koenig, *Mouse Tales: A Behind-the-Ears Look at Disneyland* (Irvine, CA,
1994); Peter Schweizer and Rochelle Schweizer, *Disney: The Mouse Betrayed*
(Washington, DC, 1998).

18 Carl Hiaasen, *Team Rodent: How Disney Devours the World* (New York, 1998), p. 29.

19 'Disney Slams Mouse Orgy at Paris Park', *Mail & Guardian Online* (13 October
2006), www.mg.co.za/articlepage.aspx?area=/breaking_news/other_news=/
&articleid=286576.

20 Elizabeth Lesly Stevens, 'Mousekefear', *Brill's Content* (December 1998/January
1999), p. 96.

21 Katie Hafner, 'Seeing Corporate Fingerprints in Wikipedia Edits', *New York Times*
(19 August 2007).

22 Gilles Deleuze and Félix Guattari, *Kafka: Toward a Minor Literature* (Minneapolis,
MN, 1986).

23 For more on theme park watchers see Scott A. Lukas, 'Signal 3: Ethnographic
Experiences in the American Theme Park Industry' (PhD dissertation Rice
University, 1998), and Marla Dickerson, 'Self-Styled Keepers of the Magic
Kingdom', *Los Angeles Times* (12 September 1996), pp. A1, 24.

24 For one example of such a homemade ride, see Oklahoma Land Run, www.jere-
myreid.com (accessed 15 January 2008).

25 In the episode 'Duff Gardens' a similar corporate parody is made. In this case,
Duff Land refers to a theme park that, like Busch Gardens, has connections to the
beer industry. A commercial for the park describes the 'happiest fish in the world'

in the Beerquarium, where fish get drunk and slam themselves against the walls of the aquarium. The park also includes a Hall of Presidents, based on beer, and an electrical parade, both of which seem like take-offs of Disney theme parks.

26 Julian Barnes, *England, England* (New York, 2000).

27 *Ibid.*, p. 189.

28 *Ibid.*, p. 188.

29 *Ibid.*, p. 259.

30 Jean Baudrillard, *Simulations* (New York, 1983). Walter Benjamin, 'The Work of Art in the Age of Its Technological Reproducibility: Second Version', in *Walter Benjamin: Selected Writings, Volume 3: 1935–1938* (Cambridge, MA, 2002).

31 Mitch Albom, The *Five People You Meet in Heaven* (New York, 2003).

32 Stanley Elkin, *The Magic Kingdom* (New York, 1985).

33 For more on theme parks as a site of therapy see Leslie Wright, 'Students Get on Road to Recovery', *Los Angeles Times* (20 December 1995), pp. A3, 26.

34 Marshall Berman, *All That Is Solid Melts Into Air: The Experience of Modernity* (New York, 1988), p. 15.

35 Patricia Leigh Brown, 'In Fairy Dust, Disney Finds New Realism', *New York Times* (20 July 1989).

36 Remarks by the President to airline employees, O'Hare International Airport (27 September 2001), www.whitehouse.gov/news/releases/2001/09/20010927-1.html (accessed 15 January 2008). Thanks to Diane Lewis (Lake Tahoe Community College Library) for locating this source.

37 Chisun Lee, 'Open-and-Shut Cases', *Village Voice* (4–10 September 2002).

38 Andrés Martinez, 'Editorial Notebook; Code Orange at Disneyland', *New York Times* (11 February 2003).

39 Sean Mussenden and Henry Pierson Curtis, 'No-Fly Zones Shield Disney's Resorts', *Orlando Sentinel* (11 May 2003). Interestingly the authors claim that Disney used the concerns about terrorism to rid its airspace of often annoying advertising planes.

40 There is a sub-literature of books aimed at children at teens that reflects a further fascination with terrorism and theme parks. One example is Eric Wilson, *Disneyland Hostage* (Minneapolis, MN, 2001). In Wilson's book the narrative takes an approach not unlike the US administration's war on terror: a girl and her mother travel to Disneyland and are interrupted by Latin American terrorists who take over the theme park for political reasons.

41 For more on these training approaches see Scott A. Lukas, 'How the Theme Park Gets Its Power: Lived Theming, Social Control, and the Themed Worker Self', in Lukas, *The Themed Space.*

42 Charles T. Powers and Bill Hazlett, 'Disneyland Closed 6 Hours Early by Longhair Invasion', *Los Angeles Times* (7 August 1970), p. 1.

43 Jacques Derrida, *Of Grammatology* (Baltimore, MD, 1997), p. 163.

44 'Cabela's Company History: Unending Progress and Growth since 1961', at www.cabelas.com/cabelas/en/templates/community/aboutus/history.jsp?auPage=history.

Select Bibliography

Adams, Judith A., *The American Amusement Park Industry* (Boston, MA, 1991)

Bégout, Bruce, *Zeropolis: The Experience of Las Vegas* (London, 2003)

Braithwaite, David, *Fairground Architecture: The World of Amusement Parks, Carnivals, and Fairs* (New York, 1968)

Cartmell, Robert, *The Incredible Scream Machine: A History of the Roller Coaster* (Fairview Park, OH, 1988)

Carver, Francisco Asensio, *Theme and Amusement Parks* (New York, 1997)

Davis, Susan G., *Spectacular Nature: Corporate Culture and the Sea World* [sic] *Experience* (Berkeley, CA, 1997)

Dunlop, Beth, *Building a Dream: The Art of Disney Architecture* (New York, 1996)

Findlay, John M., *Magic Lands: Western Cityscapes and American Culture After 1940* (Berkeley, CA, 1992)

Fjellman, Stephen M., *Vinyl Leaves: Walt Disney World and America* (Boulder, CO, 1992)

Foglesong, Richard E., *Married to the Mouse: Walt Disney World and Orlando* (New Haven, CT, 2001)

Francaviglia, Richard V., *Main Street Revisited: Time, Space, and Image Building in Small-Town America* (Iowa City, IA, 1996)

Franci, Giovanna, *Dreaming of Italy: Las Vegas and the Virtual Grand Tour* (Reno, NV, 2005)

Frantz, Douglas and Catherine Collins, *Celebration U.S.A.: Living in Disney's Brave New Town* (New York, 1999)

Gottdiener, Mark, *The Theming of America: American Dreams, Media Fantasies, and Themed Environments*, 2nd edn (Boulder, CO, 2001)

Handler, Richard and Eric Gable, *The New History in an Old Museum: Creating the Past at Colonial Williamsburg* (Durham, NC, 1997)

Herwig, Oliver and Florian Holzherr, *Dream Worlds: Architecture and Entertainment* (Munich, 2006)

Hiaasen, Carl, *Team Rodent: How Disney Devours the World* (New York, 1998)

Immerso, Michael, *Coney Island: The People's Playground* (New Brunswick, NJ, 2002)

Jaschke, Karin and Silke Ötsch, eds, *Stripping Las Vegas: A Contextual Review of Casino Resort Architecture* (Weimar, 2003)

Kasson, John F., *Amusing the Million: Coney Island at the Turn of the Century* (New York, 1978)

Klein, Norman, *The Vatican to Vegas: A History of Special Effects* (New York, 2004)

Klingmann, Anna, *Brandscapes: Architecture in the Experience Economy* (Cambridge, MA, 2007)

Koenig, David, *Mouse Tales: A Behind-the-Ears Look at Disneyland* (Irvine, CA, 1994)

Koolhaas, Rem, *Delirious New York* (New York, 1994)

Kyriazi, Gary, The *Great American Amusement Parks* (Secaucus, NJ, 1978)

Lainsbury, Andrew, *Once Upon an American Dream: The Story of Euro Disneyland* (Lawrence, KS, 2000)

Lukas, Scott A., ed., *The Themed Space: Locating Culture, Nation, and Self* (Lanham, MD, 2007)

Mangels, William F., *The Outdoor Amusement Industry: From Earliest Times to the Present* (New York, 1952)

Marling, Karal Ann, ed., *Designing Disney's Theme Parks: The Architecture of Reassurance* (Paris, 1997)

McCullough, Edo, *Good Old Coney Island: A Sentimental Journey into the Past* (New York, 2000)

Mikunda, Christian, *Brand Lands, Hot Spots and Cool Spaces: Welcome to the Third Place and the Total Marketing Experience* (London, 2004)

Mitrasinovic, Miodrag, *Total Landscape, Theme Parks, Public Space* (Burlington, VT, 2006)

Onosko, Tim, *Fun Land U.S.A.* (New York, 1978)

Oliver Pilat and Jo Ranson, *Sodom By the Sea: An Affectionate History of Coney Island* (Garden City, NY, 1941)

Project on Disney, *Inside the Mouse: Work and Play at Disney World* (Durham, NC, 1995)

Raz, Aviad E., *Riding the Black Ship: Japan and Tokyo Disneyland* (Cambridge, MA, 1999)

Register, Woody, *The Kid of Coney Island: Fred Thompson and the Rise of American Amusements* (Oxford, 2001)

Ritzer, George, *Enchanting a Disenchanted World: Revolutionizing the Means of Consumption* (Thousand Oaks, CA, 1999)

Sorkin, Michael, ed., *Variations on a Theme Park* (New York, 1992)

Venturi, Robert, Denise Scott Brown and Steven Izenour, *Learning From Las Vegas: The Forgotten Symbolism of Architectural Form*, Revised edition (Cambridge, MA, 1993)

Wasserman, Louis. *Merchandising Architecture: Architectural Implications and Applications of Amusement Themeparks* (Sheboygan, WI, 1978)

Young, Terence and Robert Riley, eds, *Theme Park Landscapes: Antecedents and Variations* (Washington, DC, 2002)

Zukin, Sharon, 'Learning from Disney World,' in *The Culture of Cities* (Malden, MA, 1995)

Acknowledgements

During the course of my work on the book, I am grateful to the many individuals who answered queries, including those in theme park public relations departments. Especially helpful in this regard were Woody Register (Sewanee: The University of the South) for his historical knowledge of Coney Island amusement parks and Lisa Foley and Diane Lewis (LTCC Library) for their archival assistance. I also owe thanks to the following for their assistance with image research: Wendy Hurlock Baker (Archives of American Art, Smithsonian Institution); Chad Boutte (Star Trek: The Experience); Melanie Davies (Holy Land Experience); Sandra Dempsey (Camelot Theme Park); Leslie Green (Smithsonian American Art Museum); Lisa Holroyd (Universal Orlando Resort); David N. Johnson (Assistant General Counsel, Hallmark Cards); Gabriele Klink (Imagine Global Communications); Crystal Kranz (LEGOLAND California); Matthew Labunka (Atari); Barbara G. Lowery (Holy Land Experience); Becky Miller (Getty Images); Kathleen Mylen-Coulombe (Yale University Art Gallery); Jane K. Newell (Anaheim Public Library); Autumn Nyiri (Museum of the City of New York); Cindy Sarko (Busch Gardens); Jeffrey A. Siebert (Schlitterbahn Waterparks); Jessica Sonders (Whitney Museum of American Art); Jim Stellmack (Great America/Gilroy Gardens); Matt Thompson (Trimedia Harrison Cowley); Patricia M. Virgil (Buffalo and Erie County Historical Society); Kimberly D. Waldman (AP Images); Paula Werne (Holiday World & Splashin' Safari); and Susan Willis (Duke University).

Special thanks are also due to my editor Vivian Constantinopoulos, whose keen knowledge of architecture and popular culture was invaluable throughout the writing of this book. I am particularly grateful for her suggestions about branding and theme parks. Thanks are also due to editor Martha Jay, who provided valuable insights on the writing. Also significant were the many fine co-workers at the now-defunct Six Flags AstroWorld, and, most of all, all of the anonymous theme park watchers who continue to inform my views of the theme park objekt.

Photo Acknowledgements

The author and publishers wish to express their thanks to the below sources of illustrative material and/or permission to reproduce it:

Photos courtesy of the Anaheim Public Library: pp. 174 (right), 181; photo AP Images/ Gautam Singh: p. 213; photos © Atari, Inc.: pp. 228, 229; photos by the author: pp. 36, 59 (right), 197, 206, 208, 215, 238, 243; author's collection: pp. 22, 28, 39, 42, 45, 47, 55, 56, 59 (left), 61, 66, 70, 73, 84, 102, 107, 108, 109, 121, 123, 128, 131, 174 (left); reprinted from the 1903 Luna Park official program (author's collection): pp. 34, 135; photo George Grantham Bain/Library of Congress (LC-DIG-ggbain-03960); © Batoots/Dreamstime.com: p. 6; photo © Daniel Boiteau/Dreamstime.com: p. 78; photo © Michael Braun/ 2008 iStock International Inc.: p. 230; photo © Jonathan Brizendine, Dreamstime.com: p. 112; photos © 2007 Busch Entertainment Corporation: pp. 111, 138, 140, 154, 156; reprinted from *Chicago Tribune Glimpses of the World's Fair* (Chicago, 1893): pp. 12, 29, 31; photo William Dayton/ Flickr: p. 163; photos Dickens World: p. 164; © Thad Donovan: pp. 11, 117, 119, 159; photo © Vito Elefante/Dreamstime.com: p. 169; photo © Joy Fera, Dreamstime.com: p. 153; photo © Ceneri/2008 iStock International Inc.: p. 100; photo © Holiday World: p. 88; photos The Holy Land Experience (Orlando, FL): pp. 149, 150; photo jimg944/Flickr p. 86; photo Jorvik Viking Centre: p. 166; photo kinderpat/Flickr p. 69: photo © Manuela Klopsch, Dreamstime.com: p. 146; photos Legoland California LLC: pp. 170, 194; Library of Congress, Washington, DC: pp. 14 (LC-USZ62-21467A), 44 (LC-USZC2-157), 48 (LC-USZ62-115623), 53 (LC-DIG-ggbain-12950), 54 (LC-USZ62-66520), 58 (LC-USZ62-55753), 63 (LC-USZ62-64286, LC-USZ62-64287), 98 (LC-DIG-ggbain-12948), 99 (LC-USZ62-19961), 129 (LC-DIG-ppmsc-08013), 136 (LC-DIG-ppmsca-12027), 143 (LC-USZ62-102884), 147 (LC-B2-2686-13), 161 (LC-DIG-ggbain-03959), 178 (LC-USZ62- 83262); photo © Carla Lisinski/2008 iStock International Inc.: p. 232; photo Manchu/Flickr: p. 18; photo Megapixie: p. 202; photo mujah/Flickr: p. 168; photo © Nsmgold/Dreamstime.com: p. 81; photo © Cora Reed, Dreamstime.com: p. 103; photo © Dave Riganelli, Dreamstime.com: p. 145; photo © Schlitterbahn: p. 43; photo Shht!/Flickr: p. 200; photos Star Trek Experience, Paramount Parks: pp. 173, 185; photo © Joanna Szycik, Dreamstime.com: p. 105; photo © ThreeJays/2008 iStock International Inc.: p. 76; Tivoli Gardens (Ellen Dahl): p. 26; photos © 2007 Universal Orlando, all rights reserved: pp. 90,

Index

ABC News 224
accidents 113, 117, 118
adult theme park 19, 167, 170, 216
The Adventures of Tom Sawyer 157
Albom, Mitch 234
Allen, John 113
Alton Towers 14, 227
American Coaster Enthusiasts 110, 114
American dream 30
Americana 93
amusement park 37, 65, 98, 132, 180, 187, 216
Amusement Park 219
amusement world picture 53
Ancona, Xavier López 175
Anheuser Busch 190, 225
animals 17, 40, 43–4, 46, 99–100, 101, 112, 120, 131, 141, 142–7, 155, 157, 189, 190, 191, 243–4
anthropology 109
archaeology 167
Archäologischer Park Carnuntum 16
architecture 9, 13, 14, 21, 23, 28, 29, 30, 32, 35, 38, 40, 50, 51, 52–3, 54, 57, 58, 63, 66, 67, 68, 69–71, 74, 77, 79, 80, 85, 95–6, 101, 104, 120, 124, 137–41, 145, 154, 159, 160, 167, 168, 170, 178, 179, 199, 207, 209, 236, 240
Aristotle 148
artificial intelligence 106

artificiality 22
Ashbury Park 174
assessment 111
AstroWorld 113, 117, 132, 156, 179–80, 192–3, 223, 225, 237
attendance 14, 56, 223
audio-animatronics 75, 121–2, 126, 145, 182
Australia 17
Austria 16, 25
automobile 64, 187

Bambi (1942) 144
Banksy 239, *239*
Barnes, Julian 231, 232
Barnum, P. T. 45
Barthes, Roland 141
Batman 193
Baudrillard, Jean 110, 139, 182, 212, 233
Beacon Tower 57
Beaux-Arts 51, 57
Belgium 16
Bellagio 51–2, 55
Benjamin, Walter 27–8, 233
Bennett, Tony 72
berm 46, 68, 151, 173, 179
Berman, Marshall 235
Big Thunder Mountain Railroad 114, 185, 239
biography 92, 94, 190–91
black box aesthetics 110, 116, 117, 121

Blackpool 14, *129*, 130–3, 187
Bobbejaanland 16, 42
Bottoms, Timothy 218
boutique space 184
Boyton, Captain Paul 41–4, 144, 146,
    213, 216
brand 10, 37, 74, 83, 151, 168, 172–211
breakdown 119–20
bricolage 225
Bryman, Alan 217, 230
Brynner, Yul 219
Burnham, Daniel 147
Busch Gardens Europe 30, 44, 49, 83, *111,
    138,* 138–9, *140,* 141, 147, *154, 156*
Bush, George W. 236

Cabela's 243–4, *243*
Caillois, Roger 137
Camelot Theme Park 15
capitalism 15, 58, 59, 64, 212
carousel 99–102, 111
Carstensen, George 26
cartoon 175
catharsis 148
Cedar Point 14, 27, 116, 221
Celebration, Florida 210
celebrity 191, 201
Centennial International Exhibition
    (1876) 37–8
Central Park 160, 179
Century 21 Exposition (1962) 35
Chicago Railroad Fair (1948) 77
children 19, 169, 174–7, 183, 192, 193,
    231, 234–5, 244
Children's Fairyland 77
Childs, Lincoln 219
China 13, 17, 25, 84–6, 88, 185, 204–5
Chinese Ethnic Culture Park 30, 85, 152
Cinderella Castle 32, 78, 140, 185, 196,
    224
cinema 8, 10, 16, 26, 46, 65, 66, 89, 90,
    95, 125, 126, 134, 154, 157, 182,
    184, 185, 193, 222, 234, 236, 242
circus 53, 142

Circus Circus 52, 169
citation 34
City Beautiful movement 30
civilizing process 179, 180, 237, 238
Civilwarland in Bad Decline 215
CNN 112, 244
Cody, Buffalo Bill 50
Comcast 229–30
commodity 27–8
conceptual travel 65, 66
Coney Island 7, 9, 12, *14,* 20, 24, 27, *28,*
    31, 34, 35, *36,* 37–64, *39, 42,* 65–6,
    70, 71, 74, 75, 80, 95, 98, *98, 114,*
    118, 120, 127–30, 134, 135, 142, *143,*
    147, 148, 167, 169, 171, 179, 180,
    182, 187, 204, 210, 212, 240
controversy 196, 198, 214
copy 25, 43, 51, 56, 60, 83, 185, 186,
    187, 225, 233
corporation 176
corporeality 133, 137
Couney, Doctor Martin 59, 134
counterfeit 25
Crash Cafe 214
Crichton, Michael 219
critic 21, 31, 71, 86, 96, 130, 131, 166,
    196, 216, 217, 218, 220, 234, 239
crowd 47, 48, 62, 106, 135, 151, 240
Crystal Beach Cyclone 109
cultural imperialism 197
culture 16, 17, 68, 69–70, 71, 95, 96,
    138, 163, 167, 197, 204, 214, 230,
    241
Curtis, Wayne 139
cybernetics 25, 49, 60, 105–6

dark ride 122–6
dark tourism 108
Dave & Buster's 200
Davis, Susan G. 146
death 109, 113, 118, 141, 218, 221
Debord, Guy 172
deep play 218
Democracity 32, 33

democracy 41, 160, 225, 236
Dentzel 101
Derrida, Jacques 23
designer 115, 219, 227
Dickens, Charles 165-7
Dickens World 93, *164*, 165-7
différance 23
Discovery Channel Flagship 200
Disney 7, 14, 28, 30, 32, 33, 39, 46, 49,
    114, 126, 129, 132, 148, 153, 159,
    160, 161, 169, 177, 181, 183, 185,
    186, 187, 194, 198, 204, 209-10, 217,
    222, 223, 224, 225, 235
Disneyization 21, 209, 217, 230
Disneyland 9, 12, 26, 32, 37, 42, 74-80,
    82, 86, 95, 114, 121, 130, 133, 145,
    157, 171, 172, 174, 175, *181*, 182,
    185, 187, 196, 203, 207, 208, 221,
    224, 236, 238, 239
Disneyland Resort Paris 16, 140-41, 175,
    196-8, 224
DisneyQuest 75
Disney, Walt 26, 33, 42, 47, 57, 63,
    74-80, 94, 95, 121, 122, 130, 140,
    142, 144, 145, 158, 168, 171, 172, 174,
    176, 177, 180, 182, 192, 199, 216
Disney's America 214
Disney's Animal Kingdon 17, 44, 89,
    144, 145, 146
Disney's California Adventure Park *81*,
    114
Disney's Hollywood Studios 89
documentary 117, 234
Dollywood 30, 35, 42, 92-5, *92*, 139, 147,
    190, 191
Donald Duck 192
Donovan, Thad *11*, *117*, 119, *119*, *159*
Dracula World 214
dramaturgy 79, 148, 158-62, 241
Dreamland 9, 27, 34, 37, 46, 57-64, *59*,
    60, *61*, *63*, 68, 69, 75, 79, 82, 88, 91,
    161, 162, 182, 207
Dreamworld 17
Dundy, Elmer 49-57, 59, 213, 216

Earth, Life, and Man 109-10
Ebsen, Buddy 122
Eco Alberto Park 15
Eco, Umberto 178
Eden Camp 15
Edison, Thomas 143
edutainment 16, 175, 176, 177
Efteling 16
Eisner, Michael 224
Elephant Hotel 39-40
Elitch Gardens 187
Elkin, Stanley 234-5
employees 104, 117, 118, 132, 140, 141,
    156-60, 180, 222, 223, 225, 237
England, England 231-3
Epcot 32, 33, 52, 69, 133, 195, 222
ESPN Zone 200, 201
ethnicity 85
ethnology 28, 45, 62, 72, 82, 121, 134,
    162-3
Europa-Park 16
Europe 16, 70, 139
everyday life 9, 51, 56, 66, 84, 115,
    126-7, 150, 154, 162, 168, 216, 217,
    236, 245
Excalibur 52
existentialism 112, 113, 118, 148, 180,
    234, 237
Exposition Universelle (1867) 27

Fabio 141, 162
family 75, 80, 115, 130, 183, 210, 211,
    233, 241
FASTPASS 106
Feltman, Charles 40
Ferris wheel 11, 30, 38, 93
Fighting the Flames 61, 82, 118
Final Destination 3 (2006) *223*, 236
fire 49, 61, 63, 93
Fire and Flames 61, 82
fireworks 23, 24, 41
The Five People You Meet in Heaven
    221, 234
flagship store 201, 204, 205

Flickr 203
food 23, 40, 94, 153, 176, 179
Forest Lawn Memorial Park 79
France 16, 67–8, 196–7
franchise 56, 179, 207
Frascati Gardens 108
Freedomland 68, 82–3, *84*, 88, 93, *107*
Freud, Sigmund 154
Frontline 146
funny face 47, 174
Futureworld (1976) 219, 220

Geertz, Clifford 218
geography 23, 25, 34, 45, 46, 65–96,
    102–6, 159, 181, 240
Germany 15–16, 202–3
Gesamtkunstwerk 56
G-Force 109, 110
ghost 126, 221–2
Giroux, Henry A. 177
Global Village 16
Goldberger, Paul 160, 199
Gold Reef City 17
Gorky, Maxim 21, 22
Graham, Billy 172
Grand Tour 65, 170
Guantanamo Bay 239
guidebooks 106
Gumpertz, Samuel 62, 162

Handwerker, Nathan 40
Happy Valley 17, 84
Hard Rock 195
Harry Potter 187–90
Haunted Mansion 75, 76, 126, 183, 210,
    221
Heide-Park 16
Herschell 101
Hersheypark 195
hidden Mickey 175
history 82, 83, 88, 94, 95, 101, 111, 132,
    133, 150, 163
Hitler, Adolf 88, 212–14
Hitler's Cross 212–14, *213*

Holiday Park 15–16
Holiday World 14, 86–8, *88*
holism 26, 53, 171, 242
Holy Land Experience 63, 93, 149–51,
    149, *150*, 152
Hong Kong 191
hot dog 40
hotel 13, 38–40
Huis Ten Boch *18*
Huizinga, Johan 137
Hummer *18*

ice slide 107
identity 28, 105, 168, 196, 201, 221
Imagineering 77, 79, 141–2, 157, 215
immersion 135, 180, 182, 184, 199, 242,
    244
immigration 15
India 212–14
Interlaken (Szenzhen) 17
Internet 9, 110, 116, 152, 166, 182, 183,
    203, 221, 222, 224, 225, 226, 227
Iraq 216, 236, 239
Iron Tower 37, 38, 120
irony 204, 207
Italia in Miniatura 16
Italy 16

Jackson, Michael 226
Japan 13, 17–18, 25, 175–7, 186, 201–2
Jaws 90, 184, *184*, 196
Jenny's Whim 23, 25
Jone's Wood 11, 23
Jorvik Viking Centre 15, *166*, 167
Jungle Cruise 194
Jurassic Park 219

Kennywood 14, 52, 131, 132–3, 187, 233
Kerzner, Sol 17
Kidzania 15, 175–7, *176*
kinetics 28, 38, 41, 47, 48, 54, 59, 98,
    101, 105, 115, 120, 124, 127, 148
King, Margaret 96
Klein, Naomi 209

Knoebels 14, 92, 101, 187
Knott's Berry Farm 12, 86, 192
Koolhaas, Rem 51
Kracauer, Siegfried 19
Kunstler, James Howard 209

La Feria de Chapultepec Mágico 15
Landow 101
Lascaux 10
Las Vegas, Nevada 7, 9, 18–19, 28, 35,
    39, 40, 51, 55, 58, 71, 78, 167–70,
    171, 179, 199, 207, 216, 236
Learning from Las Vegas 137
Lee, Bruce 191
Lego 195
Legoland *170*, 194–5, *194*, 231
Legoland Germany 15
Lennon, John 191
life form 216
lifespace 244
lifestyle 168, 196, 199, 200, 201, 204,
    205, 244
lifeworld 150, 171, 177, 191, 204
lights 52, 57
liminality 115, 125
Lindstrom, Martin 176
literature 166, 188, 189, 234
litigation 161
Liverpool John Lennon Airport 191
logo 32, 47, 168, 174, 175, 177, 203
Looff 101
Looney Tunes 180, 192, 193
loop 73, 104
The Lost City 17
lovemark 183
Luna Park 9, *22*, 31, 33, *34*, 37, 46,
    49–57, *53*, *55*, *58*, 59, 60, 61, 65, 68,
    79, 82, *123*, 130, *135*, *136*, 138,
    142–3, 148, 182, 187, 207
Luxor Las Vegas 58, *59*
Lyotard, Jean-François 91

Macy's Thanksgiving Day Parade 148
Magic Kingdom 133

The Magic Kingdom 234
Main Street 75, 77, 79, 140, 228
map 102–6, 169
Marx, Karl 235
Marylebone Gardens 24
'The Mass Ornament' 19
Mauch Chunk Railway 108, *108*
McDonald's 176
'Meet Me To-Night in Dreamland' 60
Méliès, Georges 33
memory 182, 231, 233, 234
Messmore & Damon 120
metaphor 13, 79, 97, 113, 216
method of loci 234
Mexico 15, 175
Mickey Mouse 172, 174, 175, 185, 186,
    192, 224
microtheming 78, 207, 212
Midway Plaisance *12*, 30, 72, 148
Mies van der Rohe 137
Migrant Mountain 15
Mills, Stephen F. 65
Minsk World 17, 86
Mirage, The 55, 144, 199
M&M World 200
mood 82, 89, 91, 95, 104, 172, 205
moralism 62, 64, 69, 220
'Mouse Orgy' 224
Movie Park Germany 16
MP3 59
Mumford, Lewis 118
museum 13, 17, 19, 71, 150, 165, 195, 242
music 23, 60, 94, 96, 191, 196
myth 67, 68, 116, 177

Nara Dreamland 25, 186, 187
narrative 68, 76–7, 105, 122, 126, 154,
    189, 190, 200, 214, 219, 220, 239,
    240, 242
NASCAR Cafe 200
Nathan, Robert Stuart 219
nation 46, 95, 178, 236, 237
National Historic Landmarks 116
NBC Experience Store 200

Netherlands 16
Neuschwanstein Castle 78, *78*
Neverland Valley Ranch 226
New York–New York Hotel and Casino 83, *206*, 207
New York World's Fair (1939–40) 31–3, 35, 71–4
New York World's Fair (1964–5) 33, 35, 83, 101, 121–2
Niketown 200, *200*, 201
Noah's Ark 124, 131
nostalgia 32, 37, 94, 112, 231
NRA SportsBlast 214

Ocean Dome 18, 201–2, *201*
Olmsted, Frederick Law 147, 160, 179, 180
Orlando, Florida 180, 209, 210
otherworldliness 51, 63, 66, 68, 95, 124, 130, 131

pacing 62, 126, 151–2
Paleolithic 244
Panama-Pacific International Exposition (1915) 178, *178*, 199
Pan-American Exposition (1901) 33, 122
Parc Astérix 16, 67–8, *69*
Parton, Dolly 35, 42, 92–5, 190, 191
pastiche 91
Pastoralia 215
patron 45, 49, 57, 64, 72, 79, 88, 104–5, 106, 119, 134, 135, 142, 147, 148, 149, 151, 154, 156, 157, 158, 162, 168, 175, 177, 178, 179, 180, 182, 193, 207, 210, 212, 222, 227, 237
pedagogy 62, 64, 83, 88, 110, 163–7, 175, 177, 244
performance 23, 24, 29, 48, 52, 53, 61, 67, 85, 121, 134–71, 155–8, 215
Phantasialand 16
Philadelphia Toboggan Company 113
Phoenix Seagaia Resort 201–2
Pirates of the Caribbean 76, 83, 122, 124, 126, 167, 182–3, 196, 221, 222

place 95
Plato 21, 134, 231
play 137, 218
Playmobil FunPark 15
pleasure garden 9, 11, 23–7, 32, 38, 41, 70, 102
police 238
politics 85, 214, 236, 238
Polynesian Cultural Center 163, *163*
PortAventura 16
The Prater 11, 23, 25
Proust, Marcel 231
psychology 112, 118, 203
public relations 223, 224

queue line 106, 152–4

racialism 160, 163
Rainforest Cafe 200
Ranelagh Gardens 11, 23, 24
Ravensburger Spieleland 15
reflexivity 184, 199
REI 172, 200
relationships 111, 112, 113, 115, 128, 129, 153, 241, 242
religion 62, 63, 66, 71, 94, 110, 141, 149–51, 219, 220, 221, 222, 234, 236, 242
remaking 223, 225
The Republic 21
restaurant 13, 40, 160
Reynolds, William 57–60, 63–4, 213, 216
rhetoric 94
rhizome 23, 224
ride junkies 132
rides 33, 34, 40, 46, 47–9, 50, 61, 75, 81, 89, 90, 93, 97–133, 152, 159, 182–3, 221, 226, 237
risk society 119
Roberts, Kevin 183
Rollercoaster (1977) 113, *217*, 218, 235
roller coaster 27, 40, 60, 97, 102, 107–16, 121, 218, 226
Roller Coaster Club of Great Britain

114–15
RollerCoaster Tycoon 227, *228*
Romania 214
Rowling, J. K. 188, 190

Saunders, George 215, 216
Schoepen, Bobbejaan 42
Schlitterbahn 43, *43*
Sea Lion Park 9, 37, 41–4, 65, 68, 146, 157
SeaWorld 44, 144, 146, 190, 225
Second Life 9, 229
semiotics 111–12
Send a Message to Mickey 220
senses 66, 67, 71, 100, 125, 126, 152, 153, 183, 184, 189, 199, 242
Sensurround 218
September 11th 236
sexuality 41, 48, 169, 224
Shakaland 163
Shijingshan Amusement Park 25, 185–6, 187
Shoot-the-Chutes 42, 43, *44*, 52, *54*, 59, 65, 133
shopping mall 13, 68, 160, 200, 204–5
Siegfried & Roy 144
Silver Dollar City 92, 94
The Simpsons 120, 192, 231
Sirens 168–9
Six Flags 14, 15, 47, 49, 104, 132, 148, 159, 160, 161, 187, 192, 204, 217, 224, 225
Six Flags Over Texas 9, 12, 80–2, 95, 171
Ski Dubai 16
Slosson, Edwin 126, 127, 129, 167
social class 96
social contract 179
social control 151
sociality 28, 37, 53, 115, 127, 129, 133, 160, 210, 240, 241
social organism 119
Sorkin, Michael 91
South Africa 17
South China Mall 205

SpacePort Shenyang 17
Spain 16
spectacle 24, 37, 48, 52, 54, 61, 142, 144, 148, 155, 199
Spencer, Herbert 119
Splendid China 85
Starbucks 172, 207, *208*
Star Trek: The Experience 184
Star Wars 182
steeplechase 46, 173
Steeplechase Park 9, 28, 33, 34, 37, 40, 44–9, *45*, *47*, *48*, 50, 51, 65, *66*, 77, 127, *128*, 130, 133, 151, 170, 173, 174, 175
storytelling 74, 77, 98, 125, 126, 138, 140, 141, 142, 152, 154, 157, 168, 183, 186, 189, 199, 200, 214
stunt show 48
Sun City 17
symbols 10, 12, 23, 29, 30, 31, 40, 51, 71, 83, 93, 95, 96, 101, 137, 138, 139, 146, 147, 148, 173, 174, 178, 196, 231, 236, 244

technology 32, 35, 50, 62, 72, 75, 76, 112, 115–16, 125, 126, 242
television 13, 52, 110, 157, 162, 171, 193, 222, 234
terrorism 216, 218, 236, 239
text 212–45
Thatcher, Margaret 210–11
theatre 8, 66
theme 34, 46, 69, 93, 169, 199, 229
theme land 16, 71, 74, 80, 81, 84, 86–7, 93, 194, 205, 212
Theme Park Inc 227
theme park form 96, 240
theme park nation 209
theme park watchers 225–6, 237
Theme Park World 227
theming 13, 15, 16, 61, 67–8, 70, 75–9, 82, 84, 86, 88, 89, 93, 94, 95, 98, 131, 139, 140, 141, 144, 153, 154, 156–7, 171, 186, 191, 194, 199, 201,

203, 205, 207, 213, 214, 216, 217, 242
theming complex 94, 95
therapy 235
third place 191, 207
Thompson, LaMarcus 40
Thompson, Fred 33, 49–57, 59, 130, 131,
    138, 148, 149, 213, 216
Thrill (1996) 113, 219
Thrillville 227
Tibet 85
ticket 24
Tilyou, Edward 127
Tilyou, George 33, 38, 40, 44–9, 59, 79,
    115, 127, 133, 173, 174, 175, 187,
    210, 213, 216
Tivoli 11, 23, 25–6, *26*
Tokyo Disneyland 17
Tokyo DisneySea 17
Tolstoy, Leo 21
Topsy the elephant 55, 142–3
total themed space 201, 202
Tower of Terror 222
training 8, 117, 118, 158, 237–8
Trans-Mississippi and International
    Exposition (1898) 51
travel 65, 122, 134
Traver, Harry G. 97, 109
Treasure Island (T. I.) 168–9, *168*
A Trip to the Moon 33, 46, 49, 65, 122,
    125
A Trip to the Moon (1902) 33
Tropical Islands Dome 202–3
Twain, Mark 157
Twilight Zone 126

United Arab Emirates 13, 16, 195
United Kingdom 14–15, 207
Universal City Dubailand 16
Universal Studios Japan 17, *155*
Universal Studios Orlando 7, 33, 39, 46,
    48, 49, *67*, 89–92, *90*, *91*, 95, *124*,
    126, *127*, 132, 185, 188–90, 192,

196, 204, 224
utilities 181
Utopia 219

vaudeville 66
Vauxhall Gardens 11, 23–5
Venturi, Scott Brown and Izenour 137
video games 66, 119, 122, 226–30
Vietnam War 236
vista 38, 52, 62, 152
vision 38, 53, 54, 70, 240
Virtual Magic Kingdom 228, 229

Walt Disney World 89, 180, 222, 234,
    235, 236
water 42–3, 52, 202–3, 205
weenie 199, 200
Westworld (1973) 219, 220
Wet & Wild 43
White City 30, 148
Whole Foods 200
Wikipedia 225
Wild Animal Park 17, 86
Window of the World 17, 84–5, *86*, *87*
Wizarding World of Harry Potter 188,
    188, *189*
World Park 17
world picture 54
World's Columbian Exposition (1893)
    11–12, 21, 29–30, *29*, *31*, 45, 57, 72,
    147, 148
world's fair 9, 11–12, 27–37, 62, 71–4,
    102, 120, 160, 178–9, 242
world theme park 160, 170, 209, 238
Wunderkammer 72, 73
Wynne, Angus, Jr 47, 80–1, 216

Yippies 238, 239
YouTube 226

zone 23, 29, 68, 71, 72, 102, 161
Zukin, Sharon 95, 204